Praise

FOR ANITA CARMAN

ANITA CARMAN IS BRILLIANT. I AM THRILLED ABOUT *her ministry. She has substitute taught for me in Sunday School and at retreats. I trust her teaching totally.*

BETH MOORE

ANITA CARMAN LOVES JESUS FIRSTHAND AND *foremost. She has passion for the Lord and a love for God's daughters. God has mixed these two ingredients and given her a ministry of blessing, caring, training, and loving that is infectious. We need more Anitas!*

JILL BRISCOE

ANITA CARMAN IS A VISIONARY LEADER WHO INVESTS *in women of all ethnicities. I am so grateful for Anita and Inspire Women's passion to protect the privilege of all women to be established in His Word.*

KAY ARTHUR

ANITA'S LOVE FOR THE LORD, HIS WORD AND HIS *work is not only obvious to everyone but is also contagious. Her passionate relationship with God is like a sweeping fire that causes others to burn with the same spiritual fervor. Prepare to be blessed by Anita and Inspire Women.*

PRISCILLA SHIRER

ANITA CARMAN MOVES AT SPIRIT-COMPELLED SPEED *with a contagious energy to expand God's kingdom on earth. I commend the marvelous ministry of Inspire Women!*

DR. TONY EVANS

ANITA'S LIFE, TESTIMONY, AND COMMUNICATION SKILLS *make her uniquely qualified to impact all those she comes in contact with. Her passion is highly contagious. She truly is a visionary leader crossing generations and ethnicities, bringing a message of hope. Time and consistency proves the character of individuals and organizations. The fruit of Anita Carman and Inspire Women will prove to be of great import and impact to countless lives.*

DR. DOUG STRINGER
FOUNDER, SOMEBODY CARES AMERICA

ANITA CARMAN GRADUATED TOP OF HER CLASS AT *Dallas Theological Seminary. We at Dallas Seminary are thrilled to watch how God is using Anita to inspire women across ethnicities to take the study of God's Word seriously and to apply the relevance of His Word to transform lives in families, workplaces and communities.*

DR. MARK BAILEY
PRESIDENT, DALLAS THEOLOGICAL SEMINARY

ANITA IS A FAITHFUL BELIEVER AND FRIEND WHO *desires to point to Christ in her ministry. She is helping women across the nation to live a life that honors God in the tough times and the good times. In these pages, you will find help to make through the times you want to quit or the times you are just confused on which way to turn. Let her guide you through the book of John so you can see the sun rise on the other side*

PASTOR GREGG MATTE
HOUSTON'S FIRST BAPTIST CHURCH

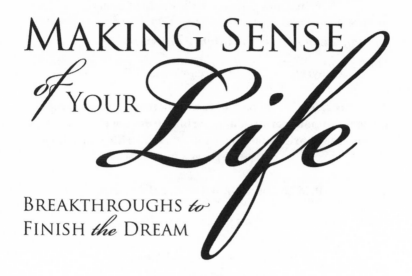

MAKING SENSE
of YOUR *Life*

BREAKTHROUGHS *to* FINISH *the* DREAM

*A*NITA *C*ARMAN
WITH ROBBIE CARMAN

Library of Congress Cataloging-in-Publication Data
Carman, Anita
Making Sense of Your Life - Breakthroughs to Finish the
Dream/Anita Carman with Robbie Carman

ISBN 978-0-9772905-1-2

Printed in the United States of America

SAN 257-1439

Published by Inspire Women
1415 S. Voss, # 110-516
Houston, TX 77057
713-521-1400

Inspire Women does not accept unsolicited manuscripts.

For additional copies of
Making Sense of Your Life: Breakthroughs to Finish the Dream
or
to contact Anita Carman for a speaking engagement
please visit www.inspirewomen.org or call 713-521-1400.

Cover design by Jenn Reese/Tiger Bright Studios
Interior design by TYPEFLOW

This book is dedicated to

Carol Ann Logan Byrd

for her tireless dedication

to grow me up

as a servant leader for God's purpose.

Contents

- *God's plan for life is in the person of Jesus.*
- *Darkness cannot snuff out the light.*
- *God wants us to follow the true light.*
- *God's plans will surpass your lifetime.*
- *God freed us from a performance treadmill.*

- *God is a parent who has proven His love.*
- *Every family's priorities are different.*
- *A location is made significant by God's presence.*
- *God knows His children and is never mistaken in His assessment.*
- *If we are part of God's family, He can raise us to be champions.*

- *When God separates us to witness a miracle, we are in training.*
- *When God is ready to act, choose the level of your blessings.*
- *At the crossroads of life, God gives us His instruction.*
- *God ushers in times of judgment as well as times of blessing.*
- *Discern God's "Now" moment of a completed miracle.*

Foreword

by Jill Briscoe

What I like most about this book you're holding is Anita Carman, the author who wrote it. She is a dear friend, colleague and fellow servant, sister in the Lord, a Jesus lover and Glory giver.

I like this book because it is uncompromising in its message, summed up in a phrase Anita uses about herself: "God's mission offers no sabbatical." What she means is that once Jesus had her heart in His hands her road was clear, and she set herself to be a blessing particularly to women, whether the "world, the flesh or the devil" tried to stop her or not! "God's plan," she tells us, "is my heartbeat, intent, and goal. It's what I'm about." And she wants us to be about the same business. As we read on she shows us how to apply the Word of God to our lives and insists we get on with it.

I like this book because Anita uses personal and moving testimony never as an end in itself, for as Paul says in 2 Corinthians 6, "We preach not ourselves but Christ Jesus the Lord and ourselves your servants for Jesus sake." So even though Anita's life story and experience is gripping and motivating it is not an end in itself, but always points us to Him who is our source and joy. In other words, it's not about her; it's about Him.

This is not an easy thing to achieve in a book. Anita, a consummate teacher, shows us how to not only study our Bible and its principles, but to get on with living a life uncompromisingly useful, and a fulfilling joy.

ENJOY!

Acknowledgments

I wish to thank my son, Robbie Carman, for helping me to finish this book. I was so overcome with grief over the gradual loss of a close friend to Alzheimer's disease that I found myself mentally and emotionally exhausted. Thank you, Robbie, for challenging me to rewrite this book based on your feedback and for taking the time to fill in the appropriate transitions and illustrations. You were God-sent at a time I greatly needed a friend. Just never thought the friend would be my own son! I pray the time you took to work on your mother's manuscript will always be one of the most special times we shared together! I will always treasure this book as one written with the help of my son.

I wish to thank Beth Jusino for her assistance in producing this book. I met Beth through my friend Jill Briscoe. Beth used to be with Alive Communications and served as Jill's literary agent. She was recommended by Jill to me as being one of the best in her field. Today, Beth is a freelance publishing consultant. I never imagined Beth would be working with me on my book. I am truly grateful!

I wish to thank Josh Vogt for serving as copy editor. Josh now lives in Denver, Colorado. He was a professional copy editor for Simon & Schuster, and has worked as a freelance copy writer and editor since. He was God's perfect choice for a book where I was writing for the general public while also creating an option for any teacher to easily personalize the principles in this book and share it with others.

In addition, I wish to thank Dr. Charles Baylis of Dallas Theological Seminary for his insights on the Book of John. Though it has been many years since I took Dr. Baylis' class, I can still hear his voice pouring out God's truths. I am grateful for the time I sat under his instruction.

INTRODUCTION

Making sense of your life

HAVE YOU EVER HIT a dead end or entered a season of turbulence where you've lost your compass? Have you ever grown weary of losing one more friend along the journey? How do you sustain the passion and momentum to accomplish a dream, regardless of how many times you must reshape it, recreate it, or redefine it?

As the founder and president of a ministry that helps thousands to discover their purpose, dare I admit needing help to make sense of my life? When I first sensed a stirring in me to begin a work of global magnitude, I was not a powerful leader filled with the confidence to conquer the world. Instead, I was uncertain and insecure about having no ready network or acceptance. I was an immigrant who came to

the great land of America at the age of seventeen, short-
ly after the tragic loss of my best friend—my mother, who
took her own life. Not exactly a great start for a teenager entering her adult years. As much as I wanted to understand
my mother's sadness, she left me with the message that I was
not important enough for her to stay.

In my mental fog, I tried to discover my purpose in life
amidst the fading voice of my mother's dreams for me. I
found an anchor in the academic world, finishing a four-
year undergraduate degree in two years and then ending
with a master's in Business Administration. I began defining
my identity in corporate America through major companies
such as Booz Allen and Hamilton and Exxon.

When I sensed God's call to full-time ministry, I completed my second master's degree in Biblical Studies.
Education, for me, was a necessity. Unlike others who God
had gifted to share His message powerfully without formal
training, I always knew I needed all the help I could get.
When I walked away from the titles and financial benefits of
a corporate career and into the nonprofit world of ministry,
I thought that was sacrifice enough. I never expected the future to require more faith and sacrifice than I ever imagined.
I have found that life is always more fun when you are setting sail than when you are in the middle of the storm and
feel the pressure to land the ship.

Basking in my relationship with God felt safe. Studying
God's Word in a library felt safe. It never dawned on me
that the deeper God develops our relationship with Him,
the more likely He will then send us into uncharted territory. We are not in preparation to sit and bask, but to go

forth and make a difference! In fact, the more we succeed, the harder the territory God will assign to us. When the call came to establish an educational ministry to empower women to use their unique gifts to serve in missions and ministry, I came up against a culture that resisted women in leadership because of gender stereotype. How could I explain that God's call to His daughters was not to seek power or entitlements, but to awaken the gifts He had given them?

My natural tendency was one of submission to any dominant voice around me, largely a result of my childhood years. I definitely wouldn't have chosen myself to be a voice for women with a passion to change the world. I was more comfortable comparing myself to the disciple John, who rested his head on Jesus' shoulders, rather than John the Baptist, whose blazing voice cried out from the wilderness. I didn't want to be a pioneer, especially considering how I loathed being uprooted from my own country. I craved community and for a place to belong. Was God asking me to create that place of belonging for thousands of women?

God didn't apologize for my lack of connections or resources while keeping to His global vision. He definitely ignored any personal protests! However, in God's mercy, He assigned me two mentors. I regarded them as my spiritual father and mother, because their role was to help me grow into a strong spiritual leader. My spiritual father met with me regularly to offer doses of encouragement. His favorite words to me were, "If you're going to dream, then dream big. You're doing great! Just keep going!" My spiritual mother embraced me as God's answer to her prayers to have global impact while suffering from a heart disease. She relentlessly prayed for me several hours a day and helped me to work through my emotional vulnerabilities and fears of rejection and abandonment. My mentors were to me like Joshua and Caleb were to Moses. They stood beside me as God entrusted me with the building of a mega-ministry.

Then God allowed me to lose my spiritual father to Alzheimer's disease. The same year I lost my spiritual father, my spiritual mother was diagnosed with Alzheimer's as well.

Right as the two major pillars in my life were removed, God also allowed others I counted on to leave. I learned the hard way the deep hurt caused by those who over-promise and under-deliver. The timing couldn't have been worse. As I wrestled with old wounds and wrecked emotions, God's mission offered no sabbatical. There were days I walked an emotional tightrope, sure it would snap, sure it required more faith from me than I ever had. If not for a few faithful workers who rallied around me, I would've drowned in my own tears!

In the movie "The Lion King," there's a scene where the baby lion, Simba, looks at his reflection in a pool of water. He concludes it's just his reflection, and an unimpressive one at that! A friend advises him to look harder. As he looks, he sees an apparition of his father and is startled into facing his own identity. His father says to him, "Simba, you have forgotten me. You have forgotten who you are so you have forgotten me. Look inside yourself, Simba. You are more than what you have become. You must take your place in the circle of life. Remember who you are. You are my son and the one true king."

I was amazed that God used an old movie to get my attention. Through the verbiage of the father to his cub, God reminded me that in the midst of all my losses and changes, I needed to remember I was made in His reflection. His purpose continues through me because no human or event can thwart God's plans. Life was never about "me against the world." Instead, life is God opposing the destructive lies of the world, by sending servants to save the world with His truth.

Did you know that God has a purpose for you that transcends any changes or losses you've experienced?

Trying to make sense of my life took me into the study of the Book of John, written by the Apostle described in John 13:23, 21: 7, and 21:20 as "the disciple whom Jesus loved." By studying the life of Jesus, I was inspired to go from basking in my relationship with God to battling for His causes. Though the image I had of the Apostle John was best described in John 13:23b as "inclining next to him," I also recalled that John spent his remaining days on earth taking care of Jesus' mother, sharing God's Word, suffering for the gospel, and writing the Book of John and the Book of Revelations. Despite physical separation from Jesus, John kept going to finish strong. I sensed that studying John's writings would help me understand and fulfill God's dreams for my life.

The Apostle John tells us in John 20:30–31 that he recorded Jesus' miracles so "that we may believe that Jesus is the Christ, the Son of God, and that by believing you may have life in his name." The life John referred to was described by Jesus in John 4:14 as a **"spring of water welling up to eternal life."**

I longed to wake up every morning wanting more of life. I was tired of feeling disconnected and wanted to get back on the same page with God. I wanted a purpose on earth with eternal significance that overflowed into eternal life. As I studied the Book of John and a few other scriptures God also brought to my attention, the dots of my life started connecting.

If you wish to connect the dots of your life, this book is for you. *Making Sense of Your Life* isn't a comprehensive study of the Book of John. Rather it's a study of seven key principles that helped me in this journey. The format of the book is as follows:

Each chapter captures a key principle from the study of the Book of John that helped me reconnect with God's plan.

- Each chapter has several questions to prompt the reader's personal application. These questions may be answered privately or shared with others during small group discussion using current or past experiences.

- Each chapter ends with my personal application of the overall principle.

- Those desiring to re-teach the materials may share the biblical content and use personal experiences to illustrate the principles. If they don't have a personal application, use mine. (Transparency helps build community and bonds the audience to the teacher.)

• To accommodate different readers' schedules, each chapter can be read as a whole or divided up into five daily devotions with a time for reflection..

• The seven key principles and the questions in this book may be reworked repeatedly as the reader faces different seasons and challenges in life. I have found these principles invaluable to get my bearings during times of change and struggle.

Are you ready to make sense of your life and fulfill the dreams God designed for you? Then may we soar towards our destination with a purpose that awakens our passion for life and overflows into eternal blessings!

1

Discern the right voice to follow

*If I find in myself a desire which no experi-
ence in this world can satisfy, the most probable
explanation is that I was made for another world.*

—C.S. Lewis, *Mere Christianity*

ERHAPS YOU SHARED A dream with a parent, a
spouse, or a best friend. What happens then when
you find yourself journeying alone? Perhaps you
had hopes to be a valuable part of a company or a ministry. What happens then when the organization folds or
reorganizes you out of the picture? Maybe you had different plans for your life. What happens when the needs of
those around you limit you from reaching your potential?

If you've been demanding answers from life, only to find silence, may the silence end today as you hear God speak to you through His Word.

If you've ever been disappointed with a dream that crashed, remember that God too had a dream that went awry. In fact, God was so disappointed in his creation that He withdrew from the world to get away from the problem. Think of the 400 years of silence between the last book of the Old Testament and the first book of the New Testament as God taking a break from Planet Earth! Have you ever been silent because your heart was broken? Did you need time to heal before you could emerge into the public again? After 400 years of silence, God spoke again. His words resonated from afar through the voice of John the Baptist, described in John 1:23a as **"the voice of one calling in the desert..."**

In the gospel of John, the first book of the New Testament, the first chapter begins, **"In the beginning was the Word."** Have you ever gone back to the beginning of a dream or a relationship gone wrong? Have you retraced your steps to recycle past promises or conversations? This time, instead of recycling your history, consider discovering a new beginning.

The new beginning that changed the world was Jesus coming to earth. This time, instead of beginning with humankind as God did with Adam and Eve, God began with His own son. Herein lies a foundational clue to the plans for our lives. We'll make sense of life when we begin with God's voice as spelt out through His words.

Imagine standing in line at the grocery store. On the checkout belt are all of the items from your regular grocery list. As the cashier idly scans your selections, you notice a candy bar on the shelf. At this moment, what thoughts run through your head? For some, I imagine the internal dialogue might go something like this:

I've had a tough day and could really use a candy bar. I don't need a candy bar, though. But, you know, my friend Carrie is in great shape and she always says that dessert is the spice of life. Then again, Carrie's already married. And anyway, candy's bad for your teeth. But how much will just one candy bar affect my life, really? The Bible does say the body is a temple of God, but I doubt eating one bar would be considered a sin...

And so on and so forth. While the processing power of our brains often allows us to reach a conclusion quickly, this kind of internal wrestling happens every day in every decision we make. In the above example alone, there are social, hormonal, health, and spiritual motivators that we glaze over in mere seconds. In real life, there are undoubtedly many more.

So, what voice are we following? That's the first thing we must figure out in trying to make sense of our life. What voice compels us? Is it a voice that sets us free to soar, or a voice that sets us back? When the Book of John started by stating, **"In the beginning was the Word,"** God set the stage of all stories of eternal significance. The Word is God's voice, both written and spoken. When we listen to the right voice, we will live out the right life.

People's words can also function as voices in our head. Indeed, words can make our day or they can haunt and depress us! Throughout the day, do certain words echo in your ears? Do you hear positive words, such as "You're great!" or "You're valuable!" or "You're one of a kind!"? Do you hear demeaning words, such as "I don't love you anymore," or "You're fired," or "We don't need you here anymore."? Perhaps you're focused on written words. Is it a love letter, an acceptance letter, or an offer letter? Is it your final divorce papers, a termination notice, or a rejection letter for a bank loan? Whatever words are affecting you, I invite you to silence all other voices and listen for the voice of God through His son, Jesus.

John 1:1–2 reads: **"In the beginning was the Word, and the Word was with God, and the Word was God. He was with God in the beginning."**

I asked myself, "In the beginning of what?" I believe God was referring to the beginning of life on earth as we know it. This earth began with **"the Word."** Likewise, our life should begin with **"the Word"**—Jesus Christ.

Imagine God's son being your beginning "word," the voice that will mark the rest of your life. Instead of letting other voices dominate your life, can you let the teaching of Jesus become the first and final word you act on? If so, then no matter what other words fill your ears, you can put them under the authority of God's Word. Ask yourself, "What does Jesus say about this?" Does Jesus say I'm loved? Does Jesus say I'm accepted? Does Jesus say I'm freed to soar? Does Jesus say He has a plan for my life?

Once you've made the choice to live under God's Word, it's equally important to figure out what His Word says. The powerful truth about Jesus' voice is that His is not an independent voice from God. John 1:1b-2 tells us Jesus was "with God." The words "with God" were repeated twice. Because Jesus was "with God" from the beginning, He expresses the heart and mind of God. In John 8:28b, Jesus said, "...I do nothing on my own but speak just what the Father has taught me." Jesus gives all ownership to God. The Father's will is what initiates all activity pertaining to God's will for our lives. In John 10:30, Jesus said, "I and the Father are one."

In John 16:13–15, Jesus said of the Holy Spirit, "But when he, the Spirit of truth, comes, he will guide you into all truth. He will not speak on his own; he will speak only what he hears...the Spirit will take from what is mine and make it known to you." The oneness of Jesus with His Father and the oneness of the Father and the Son with the Holy Spirit give me confidence that when the Bible guides me with "the Word," the Godhead has already voted. Not only do I have the assurance that what Jesus speaks is His will, but it is also the will of God the Father and of the Holy Spirit.

I recall when a particular woman joined the Inspire Women team. She said her father was reluctant for her to be in full-time ministry. When she informed him of the possibility, he started yelling. The yelling got so loud she finally left the house. I asked her to return to get her father's blessing, but she assured me it would be a waste of time. However, to pacify me, she went anyway. She said when she walked in it was like entering a different dimension of time. Her father was calm and said to her mother, "I think she should do what she wants." Her mother jumped in and immediately said, "I agree." She ran out of the house as soon as she could before they changed their minds. When she walked into my office, it was like the shackles on her life had been broken. She felt released to soar.

In a similar way, I believe our insecurity to make a decision can be removed when we have the triple vote of God the Father, God the Son, and God the Holy Spirit. They act as one. God's dream to save the world was foolproof where the Fathers willed it, the Son did it, and the Holy Spirit empowered it. So will the pattern continue in God's dream for each of our lives! We have the will of the Father, the example of the Son, and the power of the Holy Spirit to empower us in our journey.

In every journey, there's always a beginning. In your current journey, what first words or relationships mark the beginning? Are those beginning voices aligned with God's voice? Did your journey truly begin with God, or were you chasing a personal dream?

Unlike Jesus, whose beginning was with God and empowered by the Spirit, we're often marked by false starts and unhealthy relationships. But we don't have to stay stuck there. We can begin to untangle life's knots by listening to the voice of God through His son Jesus for the rest of our journey.

How can we be sure that the voice we're following is God's? We know God will never lead in a way that is inconsistent with His Word. So, one way we can evaluate what we're hearing is to compare it to the written Word. Another way we can discern God's voice is to identify what His voice sounds like. When I refer to "sound," I'm not talking about the content, but the expression and tone of His voice.

The first mention of God's voice is in the Book of Genesis. So, let's go back to Genesis 1 and listen together for what God's voice sounds like. If you have one of those Bibles that put Jesus' words in red, compare what we're about to read to His words. You'll find that He sounds just like God the Father.

In Genesis 1:2, we're told **"the earth was formless and empty, darkness was over the surface of the deep."** In the midst of this, God's voice breaks through the silence and transforms the world...

"Let there be light." (Genesis 1:3)

"Let there be an expanse between the waters to separate water from water." (Genesis 1:6)

"...Let dry ground appear." (Genesis 1:9)

"Let the land produce vegetation..." (Genesis 1:11)

"Let there be lights in the expanse of the sky..." (Genesis 1:14)

"Let the water teem with living creatures, and let birds fly..." (Genesis 1:20)

"Let the land produce living creatures according to their kinds..." (Genesis 1:24)

"Let us make man in our image, in our likeness, and let them rule..." (Genesis 1:26)

"Be fruitful and increase in number; fill the earth and subdue it..." (Genesis 1:28)

"I give you every seed-bearing plant..." (Genesis 1:29)

If you had to pick adjectives to describe God's voice, what would you choose? I would use some such as: Positive, optimistic, expansive, visionary, grand, empowering, life-generating, authoritative, generous...

So I ask myself, "As I stare at what may be a form-less, empty, and dark life, is the voice in my head positive, optimistic, expansive, visionary, grand, empowering, life-generating, authoritative, or generous? If not, whose voice am I listening to?"

For example, in God's marching orders for the ministry of Inspire Women, He impressed these words on my heart: "Establish Inspire Women as a perpetual ministry to invest in women of all ethnicities called to missions and minis-try for generations to come." Voices that argued with God's marching orders said, "But that's too much trouble...That's too inconvenient...That's too difficult...That's too tiring... That will cost too much."

In psychology, there's a teaching that espouses the power of positive thinking. A famous actor once shared on a talk show that when he first started out in acting and was dirt poor, he wrote a check for $10,000 and post-dated it. He then shared how, by the time that date rolled around, he had the money to cover the check. The idea is that posi-tive thinking causes our brain to work subconsciously to make our dreams come true. I don't know what percentage of people who think positively actually reach their dreams. However, I do know that God isn't a dreamer who practices positive thinking. Instead, whatever God thinks, He then speaks, and whatever He speaks becomes reality. God has a one hundred percent success rate. How do I know this? Because God's Word provides the evidence. Listen to the words that tell us the result of God's commands:

"Let there be light," and there was light. (Genesis 1:3)
"And it was so." (Genesis 1:7)

"And it was so." (Genesis 1:10)
"And it was so." (Genesis 1:11)
"And it was so." (Genesis 1:15)
"And it was so." (Genesis 1:24)
"And it was so." (Genesis 1:30)

So, when life isn't "so," why isn't it? Is it our own lack of expectation? Is it our lack of trust that God can overcome the darkness and the emptiness? Is it because we're listening to a different voice?

The first mention of the Devil's voice is also recorded in Genesis. Genesis 3:1b reads: **"Did God really say, 'You must not eat from any tree in the garden'?"**

The voice of the devil creates confusion and tries to make us doubt God's instructions. He is jealous of us and wants us to miss out on God's blessings.

While God fills you with His voice of hope for the future, the Devil wants to fill our ears with accusations against God. You might've heard a voice saying, "Did God really say you would be married happily ever after? Look at your life now. You've lost everything!" Perhaps you've heard these words, "Did God really say He called you to be a mother? What kind of mother are you? Look at where your kids are today!" Or, "Did God really say you would have a great career in this company? Look how you're pounding the pavement searching for work!" Or even, "Did God really say He would give you a best friend? Your best friend has turned into your worst enemy and abandoned you!" The Devil's voice causes you to doubt God's goodness.

Even if you have been deceived by the Devil's voice, you can choose this very second to start listening for God's voice.

Take heart by hearing God's voice in the situation where Adam and Eve had already been deceived by the Devil.

Genesis 3:9 reads: **But the Lord God called to the man, "Where are you?"**

Far from an offhand or innocent question, this is actually great news! It means that when we make the mistake of following the wrong voice, God comes looking for us. He doesn't give up on us. In the first book of the Old Testament, God came looking for Adam and Eve. In John 1:1–2, we see how God sent Jesus into the world to offer us a way back to the right path. Jesus was God's rescue plan to bring us safely home to Him.

Sometimes the hustle and bustle of life can impede even our best intentions to follow the right voice. One day, my husband needed to take his car for maintenance. He asked me to follow him so I could then drop him off at the office while his car was being serviced. I drove out of our driveway and was sitting at a red light when the driver behind me got out of his car and ran towards mine. At first glance, I thought, "Who in the world is that?" Then I realized it was my husband! He knocked on my window and motioned for me to roll it down. He asked, "Did you forget you were following me?" Oops. As soon as I drove out of the driveway, I had totally forgotten and was heading off my own merry way. He said, "Don't forget, dear. Follow me." Then he returned to his car.

When this incident happened, God alerted me to the many voices in our heads that fight for our attention. How easy it is to merely "forget" the voice of truth you committed to follow. Whether your thoughts are muddled with past conversations, meetings, or even the lyrics to a song on the radio, I wonder how many false starts we've had in life because we were following the wrong voice or got distracted along the way.

Even when we may have embarked on a journey without God, the great news is, God was there at the beginning of our existence. He was with us even when we were unaware of Him. Therefore, choosing to begin our journey with God is not some new concept. It's simply returning to life as it first began and how God meant life to be. God with us was always God's plan from the beginning.

Psalms 139:15–16 tells us: **"My frame was not hidden from you when I was made in the secret place. When I was woven together in the depths of the earth, your eyes saw my unformed body. All the days ordained for me were written in your book before one of them came to be."**

Life then becomes a journey of discovering the truth of God with us: God can silence the false voices that mar our beginnings.

My application

Jesus was described as the **"Word."** More than that, He was the **"Word"** who was with God at the beginning. He wasn't an independent opinion. In a world where many people say things solely out of their own wisdom, I'm comforted to know that every word out of Jesus' mouth is connected to the heart and purpose of God the Father. Therefore, I can trust it for the direction of my life. I can also trust that if Jesus' voice was present at the beginning of time as we know it, I can ask Him to be the voice in the beginnings of all my journeys.

The more I ponder Jesus being the "**Word**" God wanted as the voice in my life, the more I ask myself, "What voices do I allow to control my life?" When I close my eyes and imagine the first voice that I hear, is it a voice aligned with God's heart? For too long, I lived with voices that lied to me by painting a bleak picture of life and the world. When I think back, the first voices I recall are my parents'. I can still hear my mother tell me I was an unwanted pregnancy. I can hear her promising she would never leave me…only to later hear my father screaming for help as he discovered her suicide. I can hear my sister sobbing as she cried out, "Mom, don't leave. Tell me what to do!"

Because my mother was a dominant voice in my life, when she fell silent, I lost my compass. Yet in that time, God was telling me to cling to His words, to keep His written word as a rock beneath my feet. If I want to operate from a place of strength, I must commit to studying God's Word. Only when I know God's Word will I recognize His voice, which will be the light that guides my life.

When I worked in corporate America, I had the support of a government that required organizations to recognize and affirm women for their leadership abilities. In the world of ministry, however, the very idea of God gifting a woman for leadership evoked paranoia among some men. They were more comfortable viewing women as implementers of ideas, rather than offering ideas of their own.

I recall one particular telephone conversation that haunted me. I called a Christian male leader who had instructed a supporter to redirect his assistance away from the women. I asked him, "Why did you persuade the donor to withdraw the scholarship funds from our women?" His answer? "Anyone will tell you that if you have a dollar to spend, you should not invest it in the women. It's common sense that investing in the men will bring a greater rate of return for the Kingdom."

Thank God his was not the only voice in the world of theology! As a rebuttal to the protests to invest in women, God raised up pastors whose words were like a fresh wind from heaven. One pastor told me, "Do you remember the story of Nehemiah? He didn't leave his work to respond to those who tried to distract him. So, don't let the voices of the naysayers stop you from building what God told you to build." Another pastor said, "Please tell the person who offered me a scholarship that I would like to share my scholarship with my sisters in Christ, who also need help." As a result of this generous offer, each woman who needed assistance received a full scholarship!

Through such encouragements, God continues to remind me that His voice will prevail. More than that, He sends His friends to represent Him. God's voice at the launch of His dreams is positive, optimistic, expansive, visionary, grand, empowering, life-generating, authoritative, and generous. In God's voice, I have found my confidence. Moreover, my assurance is in the fact that whatever God has spoken, history records the results:

And it was so.

YOUR APPLICATION

Write down a key voice that affects you in a negative way. This could be a voice from your formative years, or a current one in your family, workplace, or ministry How does knowing God wants to be the primary voice in your life change how you process your thoughts?

DAY 1

Devotion

GOD'S PLAN FOR LIFE IS IN THE

PERSON OF JESUS—INSTEAD OF

TRUSTING YOUR OWN PLANS,

START TRUSTING GOD'S PERSON.

———

G OD INTENDED OUR RELATIONSHIP WITH HIM TO BE the dominant one in our lives. The Apostle John said in John 1:3–4 that **"Through him all things were made; without him nothing was made that has been made. In him was life and that life was the light of men."**

Our relationship with our Creator will define or redefine all other relationships. Since all things were made through God, He must have a master plan. In God's divine order, there's a perfect place and reason for our existence. We can discover the answers as we get to know the **"Him"** who embodies life.

So what does it mean to count on a plan embodied in a person? For example, a new bride is committed to journey with her husband through the rest of her life. In her mind, she's saying, "No matter what changes lies ahead, my trust is not in a plan, but in the person." This means having your confidence in that person's character, your shared values, and love for each other. To trust in God's person-plan means getting to know God through His son Jesus. It means aligning your decisions based on Jesus' character of holiness and His purpose in the world.

The words **"without him nothing was made that has been made"** cause me to stop in my tracks and review the activities on my platter. Surely, there have been many monuments built over the years. There have been many successes that were disconnected from God's heart or purpose. So, when God says nothing was made without Him, could it be that any activity born from my own heart amounts to a big nothing in His eyes? Why bother, then, with activities that will count for nothing in eternity? I can have the best of both worlds right now. I can choose to spend my moments on activities that reflect God's character or advance His purpose on earth. I can choose how I invest my moments well, knowing that when I live to delight God's heart my time on earth will result in eternal rewards.

My application

God's Word tells me that all things were made through Him. What are the things that are made that are not through Him? How many of my plans were born out of my own ambition, compared to God's mission? What does it mean to make God the primary and foremost relationship in my life?

When I was growing up, my mother put the hope of the family's future in my studies. She believed with all her heart that my education was the ticket to a better future. While others went to the beach or enjoyed their weekends, I was always in the library. I felt the responsibility and the pressure to succeed. As much as I wanted to rid myself of the stress, I knew my family had few options except for my success. When my mother took her own life, I was devastated that I hadn't worked fast enough to get her out of her desperate situation. God alone could appease me and alleviate my utter sense of regret. He reminded me that I wasn't created to be the savior of the world or even of my family. God sent us a Savior in Jesus because He alone could handle the responsibility.

Since then, I've learned that life works better when I make Jesus the central character and allow Him to save the day! When people try to crown me as a savior, I remind myself that they are putting too much pressure on an imperfect human being. Instead of believing that I'm indispensable, I let God's Word recalibrate my self- image. I exist for God's purpose. I operate best as His servant. He deserves the lime-light, and I'm just the support staff.

When I got married, I was late for the wedding. My husband told me that he stood at the altar, wondering if I had changed my mind. His brother, the best man, looked at him sympathetically. Everyone kept looking back towards the door for the bride. At my wedding, I was the most important character for the event because. Until I showed up, all activity was on hold. As I go through life, do I see God as the most important character? Do my activities revolve around His greater purpose? Do I ask myself, "Does God care about this? What choice would best tell the world how great God is?" Or do I compartmentalize life, do my thing, and then do my God-thing as a side item?

One time, when my sons were in high school, I took a break after producing a citywide event that reached thousands. During one of their games, a high school mom cornered me and asked me to sign up to staff the concession stand. I asked my sons if they wanted me to do that. They said, "No, Mom. That's not important to us." I declined the invitation and sensed the indignation of the woman who labeled me as being full of myself. I felt badly for a while, until God asked me the question, "Given your choices for service, which honors God more?" I could've embraced the opportunity to staff the concession stand if that was what God led me to. However, given that there's only so much time in a day, and given that God provided other open doors for my service, I chose the opportunity to introduce God to more people.

YOUR APPLICATION

Describe a recent time you fought with God and resented giving Him a say-so in your decisions. How can you settle, once and for all, who is boss in your life? Given your opportunities for service, which one helps you tell more people about God?

DAY 2

DARKNESS CANNOT SNUFF OUT

THE LIGHT—GOD'S LIGHT IN YOU

CAN STILL SHINE EVEN IF PEOPLE

DON'T AFFIRM YOU.

JOHN 1:5 READS: **The light shines in the darkness, but the darkness had not understood it.**

The Apostle John tells us that when Jesus came to earth, He was God's light in the world. Although He shone as a light in the darkness, the Bible tells us that the darkness had not understood it. More than 2,000 years since the writing of the Book of John, and life continues in much the same way. Don't be surprised when people around you don't recognize a messenger of light.

If God has given you a message from His heart to the world, remember you're entering a community that has lived in darkness for a long while. It takes time to transform darkness into light. Meanwhile, find hope in knowing that Jesus didn't allow the darkness to snuff out the light. In His example, we will find our courage to go and do likewise.

John 1:10 reads: **He was in the world, and though the world was made through him, the world did not recognize him.**

Why didn't the world recognize Jesus? What was the world doing that kept it oblivious to the Creator? From the day we were born, there has been a battle for our attention: God's voice versus the other voices. Life was no different during Old Testament times before Jesus came. Matthew 24:37–39 tells us: **"As it was in the days of Noah, so it will be at the coming of the Son of Man. For in the days before the flood, people were eating and drinking, marrying and giving in marriage, up to the day Noah entered the ark; and they knew nothing about what would happen until the flood came and took them all away. That is how it will be at the coming of the Son of Man."**

The first time Jesus came, He offered us a gift to eternal life. The next time Jesus comes, He will come to judge and separate those who have accepted Him and those who have not. In the midst of our busy lives, we are all headed for the same place, where each of us has to tell God what we did with His revelation about Jesus. So, while I can immerse myself in project after project, or attend celebration after celebration, there will still come that day when my time on earth is over. And then God wants to know, "What did you do with the message of my son, Jesus? Did you redefine your priorities based on the fact that He paid the penalty for your sins? Or did you continue life as if nothing significant happened?" According to God, all humanity was on death row because no human was able to meet His perfect holy standards. What do you think a person on death row would do with the rest of his or her life if a man walked in at the moment of execution to say, "I will die in your place!"? Now imagine the father of the son who took your place on death row. How do you think the father would respond to you when he met you face-to-face and found you went about life ignoring the sacrifice of his personal loss?

God's light came to shine in the darkness. It matters little if the darkness recognized or accepted the light. Jesus stayed focused on His mission and message. The world's response—or lack of it—didn't change the course of His life. What about you? If you have been sent by God to illuminate your family, your community, your workplace, or a ministry, did you allow someone or something to snuff out your light?

My application

God's character never changes based on circumstances or how people respond to Him. When Jesus was on earth and people didn't believe Him, it didn't stop Him from being the light God sent Him to be. Do I respond to a lack of affirmation in the same way? Or do I allow the lack of affirmation to rewrite God's purpose in my life?

Many times, in a family situation, a woman will sacrifice her own needs to take care of others'. If a woman desires to study God's Word in an accredited institution, the tuition expense is often considered a discretionary expense the family won't invest in. I believe God is offended when economic reasons keep His daughters from studying His Word at an accredited level. It's like saying, "Women shouldn't go to college. It's a waste of money." The first time I shared the vision of endowing biblical training for women in my city, I was laughed out of the room. I confess I was shaken because I was looking for that nod of approval before having the confidence to proceed.

God reminded me that when I'm sure of my calling, I persevere in it, no matter what anyone says. For example, when my two sons were preschoolers, I found out they both had a speech problem. I didn't spare any time or expense to get them speech therapy. It mattered little to me what anyone else thought. Some people said, "Don't worry. Those problems will work themselves out in time!" I wouldn't take the chance because preparing for their future was a priority for me. In my role as mother, I never asked permission to make decisions in the best interest of my sons. I even tell my sons, "I am not your friend, I am your mother. I am not trying to win some popularity contest by doing what you want. I will make the decision that I believe is best for you!"

I now realize that the times I look for approval reveal my own uncertainty over my identity. If I were really sure of what God sent me to do, I would never allow others' opinions to stop or distract me. So, is it true that the darkness can snuff out the light? Or is mine a case of my lack of confidence allowing the darkness to overwhelm me? The problem isn't the darkness. The problem is me!

YOUR APPLICATION

Describe a time you allowed someone's disapproval to cause you to be unsure of yourself. Say whether they were the real problem or if it was your own insecurity. How can you be surer of yourself in the future?

DAY 3

GOD WANTS US TO FOLLOW THE

TRUE LIGHT—CHOOSE TO BUILD

YOUR LIFE ON TRUTH, NOT LIES.

———•——•———

In the Jewish culture, a fact is established by the testimony of two witnesses. The Apostle John is our first witness. He then introduced John the Baptist in the narrative as a second witness. John 1:7 tells us that John the Baptist **"came as a witness to testify concerning that light, so that through him all men might believe. He himself was not the light; he came only as a witness to the light."**

In John 1:9, John the Baptist identified Jesus as **"The true light that gives light to every man was coming into the world."**

The fact that God's Word referred to Jesus as the *true* light indicates God was contrasting Jesus to others who had misrepresented themselves as the truth. I can definitely relate to the disappointment of finding out that something we hoped to be true is a deception.

I recently went on a quest for truth as it pertained to wrinkle creams. I joined a few of my friends who were determined to find what was on the market that worked. There were times we appeared as explorers in a treasure hunt, in search of a lost treasure in some sunken ship in the middle of a vast ocean. Oh, the hope it gave us to think we would one day land on that exact spot where the treasure hid. Yet no one wanted to state the obvious questions: What if the treasure didn't exist? What if it was all hype? What if, after all our effort, there was actually no hidden gem in the vast ocean?

Wrinkle cream advertisers and promoters continue to sell their products, claiming someone has discovered a secret formula and is offering it to the world…for a price. But, oh, the disappointment when the formula fails, and we're left with the question, "Is there anything out there that truly works?"

On the more serious topic of eternal life, God wanted us to know that Jesus was—and is—the true light. He embodied the truth, sent by God to walk on earth with the message of salvation.

Why was it necessary for God to send John the Baptist to prepare the way for Jesus? John 1:17–18 reads: **"For the law was given through Moses; grace and truth came from Jesus Christ. No one has ever seen God, but the one and only Son, who is at the Father's side, has made him known."**

What we have here is a situation where no one has seen God, and thus nobody directly knows what God is like. God solves that problem by sending Jesus to earth. Questions such as "What does God look like? What does God want us to do with our lives? What does God think about my situation?" can be answered by studying the life of Jesus and discerning what He would say about the matter. God wants us to build our future on the foundation of truth, not lies. In John 8:44, God described the devil as **"a murderer from the beginning, not holding to the truth, for there is no truth in him. When he lies, he speaks his native language, for he is a liar and the father of lies."** We can either follow the father of lies or the father of truth. God wants us to build our lives by following Jesus as our true light.

Even though Jesus came as God in the flesh, no one knew to recognize him as such. So God sent John the Baptist to prepare the way. God sent Jesus as the embodiment of truth and grace, but the people were familiar with the Law of Moses and God's judgment for disobeying the Law. In contrast to this, God's true light showed up with an aura of grace and truth.

My application

The Bible describes Jesus as **"the true light."** This tells me there can be "false" lights as well. Do I look to Jesus as the true light in my life? Have I believed in others more than God Himself?

As a child, I counted on the promises of my mother. I believed her more than anyone on earth. She represented God to me. She promised she would never leave me, and I believed her. No matter how challenging life was, we promised to be there for each other. Then, when I woke up to find she had taken her own life, I was devastated and in shock. I felt betrayed and couldn't believe she had lied to me. She gave me a false security and didn't consider the impact of her choice on my life. Since my loss, I've had other relationships with people who lied to me. Because the absence of truth left such deep scars in my spirit, I find myself ultra-sensitive to matters of truth.

When I was single, I recall how I allowed myself to be swept off my feet by a particular businessman. He invited me to lunch, and by the time I returned to my desk, there were roses and a note that read, "Can't wait to see you again. What about dinner this evening?" I believed this man when he told me he had never met anyone like me and that I was the only one for him. Then I found out he said the same thing to eight different women in eight different cities. Each one thought they were the only one. When I confronted him on the deceit, he said he had insecurities from his past. The only way he could have a relationship was to spread the risk by having several relationships going at the same time. I left that relationship feeling like I couldn't trust anyone ever again!

When the Bible tells me that Jesus is the true light, I know that deep down in the core of my being, I long for Him. Any time I am dwelling on the memories of those who lied to me, I cling to Jesus as my truth.

Your application

Describe a time you were disappointed by the betrayal (however big or small) of someone you trusted. Share how knowing Jesus is the true light restores your confidence in life.

DAY 4
Devotion

GOD'S PLANS WILL SURPASS YOUR

LIFETIME—LET YOUR VOICE

SERVE UNDER GOD'S GREATER

VOICE ON EARTH.

———— • ————

JOHN 1:14–16 READS: **The Word became flesh and made his dwelling among us.** *We have seen his glory,* **the glory of the One and Only, who came from the Father, full of grace and truth. John testifies concerning him. He cries out, saying, "This was he of whom I said, 'He who comes after me has surpassed me because he was before me.'"**

When Jesus showed up to restore His children, John the Apostle testified seeing God's glory surround Him like an aura. What does it mean to see God's glory? John connected the idea of God's glory with the idea of God surpassing us and deserving the limelight.

Imagine you're the speaker at an event when the king of a country walks into the audience. Imagine the eyes of the audience turning from you to the prominent figure whose entrance changed the entire atmosphere of the event. Whether or not you personally like that king or support the policies of his country, the importance of his position demands attention. Anyone who ignored him would be considered ignorant or disrespectful. When John tells us that Jesus had made his dwelling among us and that "we have seen his glory," it was like a herald with a trumpet announcing the royal arrival. What have you done with the fact that the King of Kings entered our world?

John the Baptist gives one reason God surpasses us. He said in John 1:15 that the reason God "surpassed me" was because he "was before me." God existed long before we ever came to be and He will exist long after we're no longer on earth. We were born to fulfill a specific purpose to forward His plans.

Think of your life as a song God wrote for you to sing. When we do our part, His music will fill the earth. Have you left your song unsung? At the same time, no matter what song God has written for us, He also wants us to know that He directs the entire orchestra. God is the one producing a symphony, and His music will continue even after we're gone.

My application

God is eternal and existed before me. Life is about God's music filling the earth during my time here and long afterwards. I have to intentionally remind myself to focus on fitting into God's eternal timeline instead of fixating on the temporary challenges in my life.

When I stare at my face in the mirror every morning, life feels very immediate. I immediately see any blemish or line. I easily get consumed with my deadlines and schedule. It takes a deliberate choice to connect my life to what is eternally significant.

One way I can do this is to invest in helping the next generation continue to honor God. (However, I also can't stress myself out by trying to plan too many life spans beyond my time on earth. How do you plan for a great great-great-great-grand child? At some point, the planning gets ridiculous!)

What I need to do is to teach the next generation God's Word so they'll have values based on His priorities. Then, no matter what change lies ahead, those I have invested in will have a better chance of making the right decisions. When I look at any one choice my sons or spiritual children make, I can get all worked up. God reminds me that the next generation will be making many more decisions, and there will come a time when I won't be here to intervene. At some point, I must release the next generation to God's hands and trust that whatever has been sown will bear fruit in its time.

So let me do what I can in my time and space to invest in my family and community and trust that they then will invest in others. Let me have the confidence to know that God is fully able to receive the gift of my life's service and manage the future.

YOUR APPLICATION

Describe a time you tried to manage details that were beyond your control. How does knowing your time on earth is temporary encourage you to do what you can and trust God with the rest?

DAY 5

GOD FREED US FROM A

PERFORMANCE TREADMILL—

SILENCE THE VOICE OF

CONDEMNATION TO LIVE

UNDER GOD'S VOICE OF

GRACE AND TRUTH.

JOHN 1:16–17 READS: **From the fullness of his grace we have all received one blessing after another. For the law was given through Moses; grace and truth came through Jesus Christ.**

In John 1:16, John said it was from the **"fullness"** of God's grace that **"we have all received one blessing after another."** When God gave us Jesus, He didn't hold back. He released what He considered to be the ultimate and fullness of His divine favor. In God's fullness of grace through Jesus, God sees us as having received **"blessing after blessing."** As you go about life, do you live as one who is blessed? If not, what voice has deceived you?

When our blessings are rooted in grace, we no longer live in an atmosphere of performance. Life is no longer about **"the law"** that was **"given through Moses"** as described in John 1:17a. Life is no longer about a performance treadmill. Instead, what God wants is for us to live in an atmosphere of grace and truth. In John 1:17b, John said, **"Grace and truth came through Jesus Christ."**

What is the significance of a God who is the embodiment of grace and truth? Some truths are not pretty. If God came only with the truth, it would be like a parent coming home, fully aware of all the children did wrong while the parent was away. A parent who knows the truths of bad behavior may be viewed angry or judgmental. But Jesus embodied both grace and truth. This means God knows the truth about our sin but has chosen to offer grace. God came to offer forgiveness even before we knew to ask for forgiveness. Oh, the freedom in recognizing, "God didn't pick me because I'm perfect. He didn't pick me because I'm smart. He didn't pick me because I'm good looking. He picked me because I'm His and because He wanted me to live with Him in eternity."

MY APPLICATION

Jesus embodied grace and truth. What a contrast to some bosses I've worked for. Since God is my ultimate boss, I need to learn to celebrate my new work environment. I was born to operate in an atmosphere of grace and truth! But what does it mean to excel in such an environment?

I once worked for a boss who didn't care about me as a person. All he cared about was whether I made the goal. If I did, I had his approval. If I missed it, I felt his wrath. I felt I could never soar because I was too afraid to fail. Then I served under a boss who encouraged me to excel while providing a safety net in case I fell short of the goal. During this time, I found freedom in trying new ideas and achieving goals beyond what was set for me. I wanted to succeed, knowing that if I failed, my boss was already prepared to make up for my failure.

When God offers me an atmosphere of grace and truth, it's a utopia for growth and fruitful harvest. Have I taken advantage of my utopia, or do I live in the fear of performance and judgment? Do I serve as the child of the King, embracing the challenge to conquer the world with my heavenly Father's commitment to cover my imperfections with His grace?

In the Inspire Women ministry, I try to remind the staff that God wants our heart most of all. When we're producing citywide events, we often feel the pressure to recruit attendees. After all the time, effort, and cost, we long for a full event. We also know our supporters expect it. However, oftentimes we cannot control what's happening in the weather or in the world. One year, the terrorist attack of the World Trade Center happened just as the ministry's publicity for a conference went in the mail. It was no coincidence that the response to the mailing was poor. Because our priority was to honor God, though, we were less consumed with numbers as we were to meet the need in the community. We recognized that people were in shock and needed reassurance. So we gave out friendship passes to those who wished to bring their coworkers or neighbors to the conference to receive God's hope. We waived the registration fee and trusted God to provide. God, in turn, packed the conference. When we didn't try to force results, but focused on simply doing the right thing, we were operating in an atmosphere of grace and truth.

Your application

Describe a time your fear of failure kept you in bondage to the law of performance. Say how you would serve differently if you stayed mentally in a place of grace.

Weekend
Reflection

MY APPLICATION

———◆———

When I began writing *Making Sense of Your Life*, I was distracted and broken-hearted over my spiritual mother's diagnosis of Alzheimer's disease.

I had recently lost another close friend—the ministry's founding spiritual father—to the same disease. What a blow to discover that another close friend would be taken in the same way.

Nancy Reagan spoke of the disease as "the long goodbye." I felt I was saying one long goodbye after another, and it was overwhelming. But I knew that God's removal of emotional pillars in my life didn't change the ministry's mission. In the midst of the deadlines and challenges of moving forward, I was serving on the outside while crying on the inside.

And despite wanting to take a sabbatical from the world, I still felt the pressure as the founder and president of Inspire Women to keep motivating those around me to live out God's purpose!

It was then that the voice of the Devil said, "You see, you're alone again!" Along with those whispers came the subtle seeds of doubt. "Did God really say you're to establish a perpetual ministry that will encourage women from generation to generation?" Everything in me wanted an exit. Surely, with two of my mentors no longer walking beside me, this would've been a great time to say the season was over.

But God reminded me His mission isn't dependent on a person. He will walk with me and bring me the people I need in order to finish.

The dream is bigger than my close friends. In fact, the dream is bigger than me. Life became clearer when I started to listen to the right voice.

Your application

Write down a current situation that has caused confusion in your life. State the truths from this chapter that gave you a different view of yourself or your situation. State how you will live differently based on the new truths you've learned.

2

Resolve a father or mother wound

There's one sad truth in life I've found
While journeying east and west -
The only folks we really wound
Are those we love the best.

—Ella Wheeler Wilcox

I DROVE INTO THE PARKING lot of the Inspire Women headquarters one day and saw one of the ministry's scholarship recipients walking towards her car. She wore a pretty blouse and her hair blew gently in the breeze. Her features were picture perfect. She looked at me with a big smile and waved. Outwardly, she appeared a young woman in her thirties, filled with a passion and purpose to change the world. What most didn't know was her background. She was raised in a home with an alcoholic father, and his erratic behavior filled her with insecurities. When the topic of family comes up, her eyes still brim with tears.

I mention her because I saw her the day I returned from attending a memorial service for the father of one of the local pastors. In the pastor's message, he shared how incredible his father was. He spoke of how his father attended his church and listened to his sermons every Sunday. It was obvious his father was proud of him. This pastor came from a background with solid roots. What a contrast to those who never had an affirming father figure or whose fathers abandoned them at a young age. Jonas Salk once said: **"Good parents give their children roots and wings. Roots to know where home is, wings to fly away and exercise what's been taught them."** But what happens when the roots have been ripped away from you? Can you still fly when you are given wings later on? Or will the wings be wasted because you'll never have enough solid ground from which to take flight?

I don't know exactly how many people come from backgrounds with a solid mother and father figure. However, given the statistics on divorce, I know that those fortunate enough to have a stable family background are rare. From a place of emotional wholeness, they can minister without needing to nurse their own wounds in the process. To those given such a background, God must require more of them. My friend, Kim Watson, said, "I am God's protected pupil to edify women who didn't get what I got."

On a regular basis, I meet many who walk around with a mother wound or a father wound. It's as if something significant is missing in their lives because *someone* significant was missing in their lives. How do you make up for the hurt caused by an absentee parent?

What has encouraged me in studying God's Word is how God doesn't expect us to deny our pain. He doesn't say, "You shouldn't long for an affirming parent." He doesn't say, "You don't need a mother" or "You don't need a father." Instead, God gives us the desire of our heart, but He chooses to do it His way. God wants us to know that, ultimately, He is our parent. When an earthly parent fails in their responsibility to represent Him, He won't leave us as orphans. Jesus said in John 14:18, "**I will not leave you as orphans; I will come to you.**" King David tells us in Psalms 27:10, "**Though my father and mother forsake me, the LORD will receive me.**"

In the Book of Ezekiel, God didn't mince words when He expressed His displeasure over some shepherds who were unfaithful as spiritual parents of His flock. In Ezekiel 34, God accused them of holding the position of shepherd, yet not acting as one. Their poor performance resulted in the sheep getting hurt. The shepherds were focused on taking care of their personal needs at the cost of letting God's sheep go uncared for. In judgment, God pronounced in Ezekiel 34:11–12, "**...I myself will search for my sheep and look after them. As a shepherd looks after his scattered flock when he is with them, so will I look after my sheep. I will rescue them from all the places where they were scattered on a day of clouds and darkness.**"

I praise God for parents who reflected God's love and support of their children. These parents have given their children a head start. As their children leave the nest, these parents can slip their children's hands into God's hands and relax. It's so much easier for children to trust God as Father when they experienced a godly earthly father.

For those who have been hurt by an earthly father, it takes a greater level of faith to accept that they can trust God the Father. One sure way to learn to trust God the Father is to study His Word and see the evidence of His care throughout the generations. He isn't a parent who is full of talk but full of action. He proved His love in the most extreme way when He let go of Jesus and sent Him to earth to die for us.

Whether you came from a wholesome family background or a dysfunctional one, God's goal is for all of us to receive Him as our ultimate parent. After all, we were created as eternal beings. Our earthly family tree is constrained by time and space, but our place in God's family tree is unlimited.

In John 1:11–13, the Apostle John tells us that Jesus **"came to that which was his own, but his own did not receive him. Yet to all who received him, to those who believed in his name, he gave the right to become children of God—children born not of natural descent, nor of human decision or a husband's will, but born of God."**

What God wants is a faith child. This is a child who becomes part of God's family through belief rather than natural birth. A child of natural birth has no choice in the matter. We cannot choose our biological parents. However, a faith child can choose to be part of God's faith family. In God's faith family, each person enters by belief in Jesus' sacrifice for the forgiveness of our sins. In our accepting the gift of Christ, God then seals us permanently into His eternal family. God won't consider us faithful just because our parents are faithful. We cannot borrow our parent's belief. At some point in our lives, we must choose to believe. In a similar way, God doesn't see us as inferior just because we come from abusive or alcoholic parents. John 1:13 tells us that God's favor is not based on children born **"of natural descent, nor of human decision or a husband's will."** What God wants are children **"born of God."**

John the Baptist was a faith child because he chose to believe God and accepted the assignment to prepare the way for Jesus. When the priests and Levites sent by the Jews in Jerusalem went to question John the Baptist, he said in John 1:20, **"I am not the Christ."** His interrogators kept at him as they probed for his identity. To the follow-up inquiry in John 1:21, "Are you Elijah?" and "Are you the Prophet?" John the Baptist said, "I am not," and "No."

John the Baptist trusted God's choice for his life and didn't try to be who he wasn't. By identifying who he wasn't, he then transitioned into stating who he was. In John 1:23b, he introduced himself as **"the voice of one calling in the desert, 'Make straight the way for the Lord.'"** Have you ever gotten greater clarity as to who you are by knowing who you aren't?

When I traced the biological family tree of John the Baptist, I discovered his father's name was Zechariah and his mother's name was Elizabeth. Luke 1:6–7 tells us, **"Both** of them were upright in the sight of God, observing all the Lord's commandments and regulations blamelessly. But they had no children, because Elizabeth was barren; and they were both well along in years."

Just because someone is upright in God's eyes doesn't always mean they will exhibit trust in God's plans. In Luke 1:18, after God sent an angel to tell Zechariah he would have a child, he answered, "How can I be sure of this? I am an old man and my wife is well along in years." Zachariah was focused on his limitations and questioned God's ability to deliver on His proclamation. Because he didn't believe that God would do what He said He would do, the angel said to him in Luke 1:20, "And now you will be silent and not able to speak until the day this happens, because you did not believe my words, which will come true at their proper time."

Now contrast the judgment of silence in Zechariah's life with the voice of his son, John the Baptist, resounding from the desert. Can you marvel at how the greatness of God completely transformed the family legacy? John the Baptist made his own choice. He emerges on the pages of God's Word as one secure in his identity. He boldly proclaims the coming of the Messiah. He stands for God even unto death. Jesus said of John the Baptist in Matthew 11:11a, "I tell you the truth: Among those born of women there has not risen anyone greater than John the Baptist."

John the Baptist testified to Jesus being the Messiah. In John 1:32, he said, "I saw the Spirit come down from heaven as a dove and remain on him." The descent of the Holy Spirit was the sign God gave John the Baptist to identity Jesus as the Son of God. How do we know this? In John 1:33, John the Baptist said, **"I would not have known him, except that the one who sent me to baptize with water** told me, **'The man on whom you see the Spirit come down and remain is he who will baptize with the Holy Spirit.'"** (Underline added for emphasis.) John said, God "told" him what sign to look for, and that the sign was the Holy Spirit.

Have you been looking for a sign to validate if someone or something is true? In the same way that God told John what look for, do you think we can trust God to tell us what to look for as guidance?

Let's look at another example of a faith child in God's family. Peter's biological family members were fishermen. Jesus called Peter out of his biological family to be a fisher of men. Can you imagine Peter's family saying, "Wait a minute! What about the family fishing business?" God doesn't apologize when He requests our service. In Simon Peter's case, Jesus renamed him to more accurately represent his new role in God's kingdom. It matters little what background Peter came from and what personality he exhibited as a result of his upbringing. God wasn't limited by Peter's personality. When Jesus first met Peter, his name was Simon. John 1:42 tells us that **"Jesus looked at him and said, 'You are Simon son of John. You will be called Cephas'"** (which, when translated, is Peter). In the original Greek language, the word "Peter" means "rock." It will be upon the rock of faith like Peter's that God will build His holy community.

What wrong image do you have of yourself based on your biological background or upbringing? What personality do you express to compensate for the environment you were brought up in? I know people who tried to be funny because that was the only way they could get attention or survive their misery. I know some who were aggressive because they always had to fight for their share in the family. Others never learned boldness because life got handed to them on a silver platter.

No matter what our behavioral patterns are, something in our backgrounds shaped us in some way. Now imagine God looking into your eyes as He did Peter. God can look right into our soul and speak our future. He will not be confined by the limitations of our biological family or by the circumstances in our upbringing. Is it time to live as a member of God's faith family and let God shape your identity and future?

If you've ever suffered from a mother wound or a father wound, then discover hope in God as your ultimate parent. Instead of grieving your losses, learn to celebrate how God uses loss to draw you to Him.

In John 1:13b, the idea of being "born of God" alerts me that there's a conception time to becoming a faith child. So, imagine God drawing us to Him through events and circumstances in our lives. Think of your search for meaning and your sufferings as birthing pains. God can use any incident in your life to draw you to Him. His ultimate goal is to reinstate us as a member of His family. From this place of dignity and royal heritage, God will give us the marching orders for the future.

I used to pretend I no longer missed having a mother in my life, until God showed me He isn't advocating denial. He wants us to bring our needs to Him. He's all about meeting the need, but He will meet it in His way. I can dig my heels in and say, "But no one else but my mother will do." However, this limits my future by my own lack of imagination. I set myself free to soar when I open my heart to God's solutions. His ways are never to give me less, but to give me more. The Apostle Paul said in 2 Corinthians 5:17, **"There-fore, if anyone is in Christ, he is a new creation; the old has gone, the new has come!"** God wants us to know that in our new birth, He is our perfect mother!

My application

God's purpose for my life begins with a new birth. Am I operating out of my biological family's heritage or out of the heritage of my faith family? For the longest time, I was bothered by my mother's words that I was an unwanted pregnancy. However, in God's Word, I discovered that, whether or not we were born "of human decision," God isn't impressed with our earthly family tree. What He wants to know is whether we are part of His family tree and representing His mission. So, I need to ask myself, "What is the legacy of my faith family?" If God is recording the activities of my life, will I represent His family well or be an embarrassment?

One way I can examine my life is by writing a head-liner story on myself and seeing what I can highlight. If

I can't find a story from my life that could make headliner news for God, could it be because my life has too little to do with Him? What could a headliner title be? Perhaps "Woman shows courage for God in spite of odds" or "Woman overcomes fear to finish God's mission." Heaven forbid a headliner be "Woman's fear kept her from finishing" or "Woman loses focus and wastes her years." I thank God I have been born into His faith family. I want to draw a family tree and write my name in it so I can more clearly grasp and start living my new identity.

In God's purpose, He reserves the right to alter our self-image. Could it be that we must first see ourselves through God's eyes before we can fulfill the reason we were created? What roles have I envisioned for myself that didn't align with God's plan? While growing up, I always saw myself as a child who needed a mother. Then God revealed to me that I had a relationship with Him that my mother didn't have. I spent more time with God every day than she did and, as He comforted me, I became His messenger of hope. When I began to operate from a full emotional reservoir, I realized God intended for me to be a source of strength to my mother. I transitioned from feeling like a needy child to being a mother to my mother. My mother was emotionally desperate and looked to me as a friend. It never occurred to me that I needed to ask God for forgiveness for the times I abandoned her. My self-image limited what I did. In the same way that Peter was called the "rock," I realize now that God meant for me to be a rock for my mother.

In ministry, I had to transition from my own self-image to the image that more appropriately fit what God called me to do—to be a voice that affirms the potential of women of all ethnicities for missions and ministry. This meant I had to get out of the shadows. I was more comfortable thinking of myself as the disciple John, who leaned on Jesus' shoulders. I loved studying God's Word. I loved just spending time with God. The idea of entering uncharted territory to make a statement for God wasn't exactly what I saw myself doing. I was surprised, then, when a seminary faculty member said to me, "You are the modern Moses." I couldn't imagine being anywhere close to that. That image meant leading thousands of people through potential wilderness to reach God's destination. It would take confronting the pharaohs who blocked the way, experiencing droughts and food shortage and criticism from the very people we were trying to bless. I didn't see myself as the Moses type.

But God didn't ask my opinion. He reminded me that the passion to change the world was one He had put in me many years ago. When I was eleven, I witnessed a five-year-old beaten by her mother in an alley outside of a restaurant's kitchen. The mother was disciplining her child for not taking care of a two-year-old brother. The kitchen boys were smoking and jeering and taking bets on how many times the mother would strike her daughter. I remember running into the house and begging my mother to call the police. She told me to mind my own business. Then, from the depth of my heart, came a passion that shouted, "When I grow up, I will…" Whether or not I preferred to stay in the shadows, God allowed that incident to leave a deep mark in my spirit. Then, in God's perfect timing, He stepped me into a place where I could work tirelessly to protect the potential of women to change the world.

YOUR APPLICATION

Some roles are forced upon us by imperfect people in our circles. Describe the roles you play in your biological family. Now share a key role you play in God's faith family. Do you find yourself sacrificing more for your own family than you do for God's? How have the roles imposed on you by your biological family limited your ability to serve God?

DAY 1

GOD IS A PARENT WHO HAS

PROVEN HIS LOVE—WHO ELSE

DO YOU KNOW THAT WOULD GIVE

UP AN ONLY SON TO SAVE YOU?

WHEN JOHN THE BAPTIST SAW JESUS WALKING TO-wards him, he described him in John 1:29b as **"the Lamb of God, who takes away the sin of the world."**

God sees the sin in the world. He isn't the kind of parent who sweeps dirt under the rug. He isn't trying to paint a pretty picture of the world on the outside while hiding sin on the inside. God is perfectly holy and He wants a holy people to reflect Him. He doesn't apologize for His perfect standards. He wants children who will grow up to be just like Him in character and values. Don't expect God to hide any skeletons in the closet!

Romans 6:23 tells us, **"For the wages of sin is death, but the gift of God is eternal life in Christ Jesus our Lord."** Before God could restore us as children of a holy Kingdom, someone had to pay the penalty of our sins. Perhaps you thought your greatest need was for a job or for a husband or for money to pay your bills or for a best friend. God sees our greatest need is for a Savior. So, imagine God writing His script for your life on a slate that is filled with old scripts and broken sentences. He must wipe the slate clean so He can record His story. First and foremost, He wants to be sure you have accepted the gift of Jesus for your salvation and eternal life. Once that's settled, then He can work out the rest. Have you noticed that most people tend to do things backwards? We make the temporal urgent and put eternal things on the back burner!

God knew full well what it would take to offer us His new beginnings. He knew it would take the sacrifice of His one and only son to pay the penalty of our sins. Now think about whether there was anything in us that inspired God to make such a sacrifice. We're not talking about giving to someone grateful. On the contrary, we were arrogant, didn't think we needed a Savior, and were often ungrateful even after understanding what God gave up for us. It was God's grace alone that made it possible for us to have Jesus!

Grace is a gift we receive that is undeserved. Grace came in the form of the "Lamb of God, who takes away the sin of the world." Jesus came as the unblemished lamb that was executed to pay the penalty of all human sin. Since God paid for our sins with the life of His son, He proves Himself as the parent in our lives who didn't spare the cost to protect our potential. He is a parent we can trust. What kind of dream do you think God was protecting for us that required the life of His one and only son? Is the life you're living worthy of God's sacrifice? From our security in God as our ultimate parent, He wants us to gain solid roots. And from those, we can grow to our full potential.

MY APPLICATION

All dreams have a price. It seems that the greater the dream, the greater the sacrifice. My brother and sister-in-law were willing to do without in order to save the money for their children's education. After my mother died, my father wanted to hold on to his daughters, but allowed my sister and me to leave the nest so we could pursue our education. When I compare the sacrifices made in my own family to what God gave up for us, I can't imagine the dream God had in mind that required giving up His son to secure it. How have I wasted the blood of Jesus by the smallness of my life and what I spend my time doing?

When I found out one of my sons had asthma, I knew that I could make enough income to hire a professional nanny. However, I also knew that I personally wanted to be the one to make sure his health needs were taken care of. I remember going to the pediatrician one day when I sensed my son was having trouble breathing. The nurse said to the doctor, "I think he is fine." The doctor said, "I know this mother. If she says he is wheezing, I am sure he is wheezing." She took her stethoscope and listened to his lungs. Then she said, "Just as I thought. He is wheezing." My son's condition wasn't serious enough to justify my staying home full-time with him. I had a choice to make, and no one else could make it for me. I didn't welcome anyone's opinion because I knew that if anything were to happen to my son, no one would grieve longer and more deeply than me. Why would I care what anyone else thought since I was responsible for managing my own pain? All I knew was that I wanted to be the one to protect his potential. The cost was my career and the dreams I had for myself in corporate America. The price was high, but I was willing to pay it.

Perhaps because my mother and I were so close, I always longed for a daughter. But God didn't give me one. Then I dreamed of when I would have a wonderful daughter-in-law or perhaps a granddaughter. Then, one day, it occurred to me that God may ask me to lay down a desire of my heart. What if my sons chose to stay single? What if they married and moved away? What if I didn't have a granddaughter? It occurred to me that God allowed my circumstances to fulfill His greater purpose. Not having a daughter gave me the time to serve God's daughters through Inspire Women. Was my not having a daughter the cost of fulfilling His dream of establishing this ministry? I had to ask the question, "Would I willingly give up having a daughter in order to serve God more fully? I lose my resentment or disappointment when I realize the bigness of God's dream compared to my sacrifice.

YOUR APPLICATION

Describe the cost of a dream you are willing to pay. Then share a time when you lived for your own ambitions and didn't remember the cost God paid for your life. How can you adjust your current activities to better honor the sacrifice of God's son?

DAY 2

EVERY FAMILY'S PRIORITIES ARE

DIFFERENT—TO EXPLORE GOD'S

ACTIVITY AND THE PRIORITIES OF

YOUR FAITH FAMILY, YOU MUST

LEAVE WHERE YOU ARE.

JOHN 1:35–39 READS: The next day John was there again with two of his disciples. When he saw Jesus passing by, he said, "Look, the Lamb of God!" When the two disciples heard him say this, they followed Jesus. Turning around, Jesus saw them following and asked, "What do you want?" They said, "Rabbi" (which means Teacher), "where are you staying?" "Come," he replied, "and you will see." So they went and saw where he was staying, and spent that day with him. It was about the tenth hour.

At a recent birthday celebration, my son shared a testimony with the guests. He said, "When I was younger, I viewed my mom and dad as merely my parents. But as I've grown older, I've found I'm able to see them not only as my parents but also as the individual people they are. I love my parents as my parents, but I also respect and admire them as people."

When God invites us into His eternal family, He doesn't want a distant relationship. He doesn't want us to honor Him only because of His right to be honored as a parent. He wants us to be part of the family business and to be His voice to the world. He wants to make us managing partners with ownership in His operations. Have you ever settled for dabbling with God's activities, compared to understanding what God is doing and tackling the challenges to forward His plans? Even if you honor God as your parent, do you like Him as a "person" and love how He thinks and what He does?

John 1:35–36 tells us two of the followers of John the Baptist were drawn to Jesus when they heard him addressed as "the Lamb of God!" Has someone ever said something about God that caught your attention? If so, did you take the time to discover more about God, or did you miss your divine appointment?

In following Jesus, the two disciples inquired where He was staying. Jesus replied in John 1:39, **"Come and you will see."** Did you know that to see what God is doing, you'll need to leave what you are doing? It may mean rescheduling and changing your priorities. It may mean accepting an assignment that will give you more time in God's Word. It may mean going on a mission trip. Are you willing to take the time to find out what God is up to?

Not only did the two disciples go and see, but we're told that they spent that day with Jesus. They weren't just curious window shoppers, but shoppers with a mission. A friend once said to me, "Some people never come home with the goods!" She was referring to those who go on a mission not really understanding what they are pursuing and what the goals are. These two disciples were looking for the Messiah. They spent the day with Jesus and came home with their answer. If you want to know God better, there is no short cut from spending time with Him. It's hard to get to know someone remotely.

My application

I noticed that my husband says one word and both my sons take him seriously. Why is it that my husband never has to shout? Then it dawned on me that, as the boys were growing up, my husband was always in their lives. His goal was to be a personal coach to his sons. As they became young men, their father's voice became the voice of a trusted coach. They know they can trust their father's words. So they take him seriously.

There's no shortcut to building trust and a solid relationship. For the disciples to discover God's activities, they followed Jesus to where He was staying. They spent time with Jesus so they could get clarification for their own lives. In the same way, the only way to get to know God is to spend time with Him by studying His Word, meditating on His truths, and asking Him to reveal to us how to adjust our lives accordingly.

My spiritual mother used to say to me, "Trust takes time." When I was hurt over someone's betrayal, she would say, "You trusted them too quickly." When I asked her why she chose to be in my life, she said, "I watched what you did. I have observed you for many years. If I ever felt I could not trust you I would have withdrawn from your life." I realized that I, too, had been watching her. If she had been inconsistent in any way in my life, I would not have trusted her as my spiritual mother.

I used to say, "I wish I could trust God more." Then God showed me the only way to trust Him more was to know Him better through His Word. I must also act on His Word so He can show me the trustworthiness of His Word.

YOUR APPLICATION

Describe a time you spent with someone in order to build the relationship. What new information did you learn that bonded you more closely? What new information surprised you? Now write down what new information you learned about God lately. What was new to you and what surprised you? How will you change your life as a result of this new information?

DAY 3

Devotion

A LOCATION IS MADE

SIGNIFICANT BY GOD'S

PRESENCE—YOU MISS OUT IF YOU

WRITE OFF A LOCATION OF AS

BEING BENEATH YOU.

IN JOHN 1:43, THE APOSTLE JOHN TELLS US THAT JESUS found Philip and said to him, **"Follow me."** Philip then went and found Nathaniel and said to him in John 1:45, **"We have found the one Moses wrote about in the Law, and about whom the prophets also wrote—Jesus of Nazareth, the son of Joseph."** In John 1:46a, Nathaniel answered, **"Nazareth! Can anything good come from there?"**

Nathaniel dismissed Jesus as possibly being the Messiah because of the humble location of Nazareth. Have you ever dismissed someone as sent by God because of their home-town? Have you given too much importance to the location of someone's birth or where they were raised? Perhaps you've even limited your own potential because you felt God could never use someone from your background.

If you are gifted with many talents, perhaps your chal-lenge is that of thinking too highly of yourself. Have you ever dismissed your calling because the location God picked was too humble compared to your self-image? For example, you might be a high-level executive. How could God pos-sibly send you to a smaller company in a city in the middle of nowhere? Perhaps the organization God is sending you to looks more like a Mom-and-Pop shop compared to the well-oiled organizations you're used to. Have you felt it was beneath you to serve in a grassroots organization? Surely someone with your potential is better suited for a more pres-tigious place!

Nathaniel almost missed meeting the God of the Uni-verse because of his personal biases and prejudgments. If you find yourself hesitant to serve in a lowly place, could it be because you are unsure of your true identity? As God's children, He wants us to discover that our greatest trea-sure is already within us. God has given us eternal life and has put us in His eternal family tree. Our names are writ-ten in God's spiritual chronicles as heirs and heiresses of an eternal kingdom. When you walk around as the child des-tined to inherit heaven, you don't have to do anything else to impress the world. Is it time to stop managing an exteri-or image and start enjoying your priceless identity as God's son or daughter?

MY APPLICATION

God didn't apologize for choosing Joseph, a carpenter, to raise Jesus, or for Jesus coming from Nazareth. When people addressed His son as "Jesus of Nazareth," God wasn't embarrassed. God is confident of how our backgrounds fit into His plans. However, just because God is sure is no guarantee that others will feel the same way.

Years ago, God called me to help an organization. No matter how hard I worked and how much my ideas succeeded, I sensed a resistance from the leadership to accept me. They had a different expectation for what a leader should look like in their organization. They weren't open to anyone who didn't fit their image. God had intended for me to be a blessing to that organization. However, if someone has preconceived ideas of greatness and won't accept who God sends, they'll miss out on the blessing. I learned from Jesus that someone's bias will not diminish our identity, but it will block the blessing they could've received.

YOUR APPLICATION

Describe a time when you experienced rejection because you didn't have the credentials, the image, or other predetermined criteria. Say whether you are still allowing public opinion to stop you from fulfilling God's purpose, or share if a community's bias has kept you from being the blessing God intended you to be.

DAY 4

GOD KNOWS HIS CHILDREN

AND IS NEVER MISTAKEN IN HIS

ASSESSMENT—IF GOD ASSESSED

YOU TODAY, WOULD YOU GET A

RAVING REVIEW?

I F GOD SUMMARIZED YOUR LIFE IN ONE SENTENCE, would it coincide with your public image?

When Nathaniel approached Jesus, He said to him in John 1:47, **"Here is a true Israelite, in whom there is nothing false."** Can you imagine walking towards God and hearing Him summarize your life in one sentence? In whatever role you've been assigned in life, would God describe you as being *true?*

Let's look more closely at what a "true Israelite, in whom there is nothing false" means. Matthew Henry's commentary in *PC Study Bible Version 5* reads, "It is Christ's prerogative to know what men are *indeed;* we can but *hope the best.* The whole nation were Israelites in name, but *all are not Israel that are of Israel."*

Romans 9:6 reads: **...It is not as though God's word had failed. For not all who are descended from Israel are Israel.**

Jesus differentiated Nathaniel as a "true Israelite" to point out that God looks at the heart and not genealogy. Therefore, "not all who are descended from Israel are Israel." Jesus was trying to reach a community where those who were descendants of Abraham believed they were automatically connected to God. Their confidence was in their genealogy, not their personal relationship with God. In contemporary terms, this is like someone saying "Of course I'm Christian. My parents take me to church every Sunday and my family gives a lot to support Christian ministries." Having parents who are Christians doesn't automatically make the descendant a Christian. We don't get into heaven based on our birth certificate. God desires from each person a personal encounter and a personal decision to be in relationship with Him.

Romans 2:29 tells us: **No, a man is a Jew if he is one inwardly; and circumcision is circumcision of the heart, by the Spirit, not by the written code. Such a man's praise is not from men, but from God.**

In addition to having a confidence in their genealogy, the Jews also viewed themselves as belonging to God based on their religious activities. What God looked at was what was going on in their hearts, rather than their attempts to impress others with religious activities. That's why Romans 2:29 referred to being **"a Jew if he is one inwardly."** God wasn't satisfied with just the outward appearance. God wasn't even impressed with those who bore the sign of physical circumcision to show themselves as set apart for Him. What God wanted was circumcised hearts, meaning a people who longed to be holy in order to reflect the Holy God they served. The motive wasn't performance but relationship. The idea wasn't, "Let me do these ten religious things because that's what a good Christian does." Instead, the idea is, "Let me do these things because God is important to me and I want to do everything I can to honor Him." God wanted a people who longed for His praise more than the applause of men.

Jesus considered Nathaniel a "true Israelite" because he wasn't just going through the motions of religion. Instead, he truly worshipped God with his heart. Not only was Nathaniel a "true Israelite," but Jesus also described him as someone "in whom there is nothing false." Matthew Henry's commentary in *PC Study Bible Version 5* offered these thoughts: "...*no guile* towards men; a man without trick or design; a man that one may trust; *no guile* towards God, that is, sincere in his repentance for sin; sincere in his covenanting with God; in whose spirit is *no guile*."

Psalms 32:2 tells us: **"Blessed is the man whose sin the LORD does not count against him and in whose spirit is no deceit."**

The bottom line assessment of Nathaniel was this: Sincerely devoted to God. This was the same Nathaniel who had made the comment earlier in John 1:46, **"Nazareth!**

Can anything good come from there?" Given that Jesus commended Nathaniel as a true Israelite, it didn't appear that Jesus considered Nathaniel's earlier comment as prideful. More likely, Nathaniel was sincere. What he was guilty of was a lack of vision. He sincerely doubted that, due to the insignificance of Nazareth, the Messiah could possibly come from there.

Jesus is never wrong in his assessment. As Nathaniel was walking towards Him, Jesus sized him up in one sentence. If you were walking towards Jesus today, would He assess you as sincerely devoted to Him, or do you only look outwardly spiritual while hiding a personal values system and priorities?

MY APPLICATION

God is a perfect discerner of who we are on the inside, no matter how we appear on the outside. How frightening to even imagine what God would say about me! My guess is everyone else looking at my life would say something that aligns with my public image. However, God sees into my heart. If He summarized my life in one sentence, what would it be? What would I want it to be?

I fear God would say, "Great heart, great commitment, but needs to rely on Me more for her emotional support." I know I need a lot of growth before my service looks more like Jesus'. Jesus always felt emotionally whole, even when betrayed by His inner circle. His was not an easy mission. Yet, He never turned back, never hesitated. He didn't allow Judas' betrayal or Peter's broken commitment to set him back. I pray that one day I'll be at that place where God can say, "Great heart, great commitment, and great emotional fortitude."

YOUR APPLICATION

Imagine God summarizing your life in one sentence. Write out that sentence and say whether there is something you need to change in your life. In addition, in fulfilling the roles God has given you, would He assess you as being "*true?*" Or are you going through the motions on the outside while resenting your role on the inside?

DAY 5
Devotion

IF WE ARE PART OF GOD'S

FAMILY, HE CAN RAISE US TO

BE CHAMPIONS—GOD BEGINS

BY BUILDING YOUR FAITH FROM

WHERE YOU ARE.

———•———

AS YOU JOURNEY WITH GOD, DO YOU PUT PRESSURE ON yourself to believe more than you are able? Perhaps it's time to just relax and let God reveal truth to you in His time.

When we are journeying with God, expect Him to lead in ways beyond what our human minds can fathom. When we are following God, He will take us down paths we never expected. When Jesus turned his face towards Jerusalem and the crucifixion, there was a check in the spirit of the disciples.

Mark 8:31–32 tells us: **He then began to teach them that the Son of Man must suffer many things and be rejected by the elders, chief priests and teachers of the law, and that he must be killed and after three days rise again. He spoke plainly about this, and Peter took him aside and began to rebuke him.**

Can you hear what was going on in Peter's head? "What's going on, Jesus? What do you mean? It's dangerous in Jerusalem. You can't possibly mean we're heading there!" Peter wasn't born with faith. Just because Jesus changed his name to *"rock"* didn't mean he acted like someone with a solid foundation. Jesus prayed Peter into greater faith. Jesus said in Luke 22:31–32, **"Simon, Simon, Satan has asked to sift you as wheat. But I have prayed for you, Simon, that your faith may not fail. And when you have turned back, strengthen your brothers."**

When Nathaniel first met Jesus, he was dipping his toes in the water of faith. Jesus began developing his faith with a recent experience. Nathaniel asked Jesus in John 1:48, **"How do you know me?"** To this, Jesus answered, **"I saw you while you were still under the fig tree before Philip called you."** Nathaniel then declared in verse 49, **"Rabbi, you are the Son of God; you are the King of Israel."**

Why did Jesus knowing Nathaniel was sitting under the fig tree cause Nathaniel to conclude that Jesus was the King of Israel? Micah 4:4 tells us, **"Every man will sit under his own vine and under his own fig tree, and no one will make them afraid, for the LORD Almighty has spoken."** The spiritual significance of sitting under a fig tree is that of a person in relationship with and at peace with God.

Therefore, Nathaniel sitting under the fig tree painted the picture of a sincere Israelite who was dialoguing with and communing with God.

By proclaiming Jesus as the Son of God, Nathaniel was saying, "Wow! You were the one I was dialoguing with under the fig tree! I can't believe it! You are God! God has come!"

Jesus told Nathaniel not to be impressed just because He saw him under the fig tree. He told Nathaniel in John 1:50b, **"you shall see greater things than that."** Jesus described the greater things He was referring to in John1: 51: **"I tell you the truth, you shall see heaven open, and the angels of God ascending and descending on the Son of Man."**

With this reference, Jesus was pointing Nathaniel back to the story of Jacob. Genesis 28:12–13a tells us that Jacob **"had a dream in which he saw a stairway resting on the earth, with its top reaching to heaven, and the angels of God were ascending and descending on it. There above it stood the LORD..."** Jesus referred to Jacob's ladder as His way of telling Nathaniel that *He* was the ladder for men to reach God. Jesus was reiterating that He was the Messiah sent to restore fallen humanity to a relationship with God in heaven.

Nathaniel declaring that Jesus was the Son of God was a first step of faith. From this, Jesus would show Nathaniel greater proof of the truth. Just because you might recycle back to unbelief doesn't take away the fact that you once believed. From that first step, God will lead you into other revelations to confirm your beliefs. He will grow your faith deeper and deeper, one faithful step at a time.

Do you fully understand what God is saying when you hear Him? If you want to know more truth, perhaps you're the one keeping yourself from greater revelations. Don't beat yourself up when you have doubts. Give yourself credit for believing. Then trust God to show you greater things that will confirm your belief. Is it time for you to take a first step of faith?

MY APPLICATION

God reveals His purpose in stages. When I want to see the entire picture, I rush God and scare myself. When I look back over the years and ponder how I ended up founding and leading Inspire Women, the answer is: "From faith to faith." I served as a substitute teacher in a Sunday School class for seven years. The main teacher, Beth Moore, used to say to me, "Anita, if it's not me, it's you." I was determined to be the best substitute teacher Beth ever had.

But one day she discerned that God's calling for me was outside the umbrella of her ministry. She didn't know what it was, but she encouraged me to follow God. Though scared to death, I trusted my teacher. So I left her class as my first step of faith. I wasn't sure what kind of ministry God wanted me to have. Then, one day I was listening to the radio and heard Dr. Chuck Swindoll speak of a Houston extension of Dallas Theological Seminary. My next step of faith was to enroll in seminary. Dr. David Self—the interim pastor at my home church—gave me the counsel that ministry is not a career. He said, "You are not writing a resume. Just go through the next open door that will help you reach the most people for Jesus." As I look back over the years, I see God moving me along in His plans. I lived my life through open doors and tried to obey what I last heard God say. As I live this way, God continues to confirm His direction and reinforce my beliefs.

YOUR APPLICATION

Describe something God revealed to you in stages, as you followed Him one open door at a time. Say whether you have been obedient to what God has revealed. Is there something you need to do or finish?

Weekend
Reflection

My application

I don't know why God allowed my spiritual father to suffer from Alzheimer's disease. I definitely don't know why He allowed my spiritual mother to suffer from the same disease. As I visited my long-time confidante and mentor, there were days she was her normal self. She would recall all our adventures and the exciting times God parted the Red Sea for the ministry. Then there were days she seemed to slip into a distant world. Life was reduced to the aches in her body she couldn't explain and the numerous medications she took that offered hope, but no relief. When I asked if she knew who I was, she would say, "Of course I know who you are." However, there were days when I sensed she was lying.

I found myself saying goodbye and then saying hello. Going back and forth prolonged the pain and kept me in a constant grieving process. More than that, every time she exited from my life, old emotional wounds were re-opened. It still baffles me why my mother's suicide when I was seventeen still impacts me today. Was it the suddenness of it? Was it the panic of being left behind that makes me afraid of any similar situation? To confront my fear of abandonment,

God reminded me I was in His eternal faith family. He signed my adoption papers with the blood of Jesus. He deposited His Holy Spirit in me as a seal of His guarantee that I belonged to Him. Superior to any earthly parent, any mentor, or best friend, God Himself is my ultimate parent who will journey with me from now till forever. If there is one thing I can be sure of, it is the fact of "God with me."

Your application

Describe your current self-image as a result of your biological family. State whether your self-image from your formative childhood years helped or hindered you in God's calling for your life. Evaluate your current relationship with your family and state whether severing some ties or setting some boundaries can help you experience the full joy of being a member of God's royal family.

3

Trust God's timing has a reason

*Nothing fruitful ever comes when plants are
forced to flower in the wrong season.*

—Bette Bao Lord

F ROM THE BEGINNING OF time, God had a plan for
the world. Not only did He have a plan, but He also
had a timetable for that plan to be fulfilled. How
confident are you in God's timing?

When we are in God's plans, He controls the timing.
We don't have to stand around like someone waiting for
water to boil. When it's time for God to move forward with
His dreams for our lives, He's perfectly able to make His
will known. Once God provides the opportunity, it will be

obvious. We don't have to second-guess His open doors. We just need to walk through them.

King David tells us in Psalms 139:15–16: **"When I was woven together in the depths of the earth, your eyes saw my unformed body. All the days ordained for me were written in your book before one of them came to be."**

Did you observe the words in Psalms 139:16? **"All the days ordained for me were written in your book."** "All the days" include days of successes and days of failures. "All" includes days of good health and bad health. When a crisis hits our lives, God isn't caught off guard. He knew the thrones He would put a king on and the thrones He would throw a king off. He also knows the crosses He will choose for us to carry.

Job 14:5 reads: **"Man's days are determined; you have decreed the number of his months and have set limits he cannot exceed."**

If you think someone died prematurely, that isn't supported in the Bible. No one ever dies too young or too early. God knows from the beginning how many days each of us has on earth.

Since God ordained the number of days we would have, this tells us God didn't put us on earth randomly. He gives each person a background with a different set of talents. He put us in a certain place at a certain time because there is something He wants us to accomplish.

In your urgency to make something happen, is your motive to serve God's plans? Or are you seeking to serve your own plans? Perhaps you're desperate to show the world you can succeed. So, you're compelled by your need to prove yourself instead of submitting to whatever God needs you to do. Perhaps someone hurt you, and you feel that you will get satisfaction by succeeding. It's your way to say, "Look, I don't need you! I can make it all by myself!" Maybe you're tired of the challenges and just want to wrap up the project so you can move on to something less stressful. If so, you've given God a deadline!

God will not allow Himself to be used for our personal agenda. God will check our motive. For those who serve Him, the Bible tells us that God will give us the desires of our hearts.

Psalms 145:19 reads: **He fulfills the desires of those who fear him; he hears their cry and saves them.**

Psalms 37:4 reads: **Delight yourself in the LORD and he will give you the desires of your heart.**

When we are living in God's timing, we have everything He intended us to have for our season. When God says "No," instead of walking away feeling like God is against you, have the confidence to inquire, "Is it a 'No' to the timing but a 'Yes' to the request? Is it a 'No' to my suggested methodology but a 'Yes' to the end result?" Settle in your heart that God is for you. From this place of security, keep moving forward in your life in ways that align with God's holy character and purpose.

When you desire something good, then be assured that you and God want the same thing. God is all about goodness. God delights in showing off His goodness. He loves to work miracles that express His goodness. However, He works in His timing because He wants to maximize the good He does. If He says "No" to something you believe is good, be assured He is saying "Yes" to a good that far exceeds what you envisioned. Do you want a greater good that impacts more than your personal circumstances? How much do you want your life to be part of something bigger and better than what you imagined?

Let's gain greater insight about God's timing from the life of Mary, the mother of Jesus.

John 2:1–3 reads: **On the third day a wedding took place at Cana in Galilee. Jesus' mother was there, and Jesus and his disciples had also been invited to the wedding. When the wine was gone, Jesus' mother said to him, "They have no more wine."**

The town where the wedding took place was called "Cana in Galilee" to distinguish it from the Old Testament town of "Kanah." When God's chosen people entered the promise land, He divided the land and distributed it to the tribes of Israel. The tribe of Asher received the town of Kanah.

Josh 19:24–31 tells us: **The fifth lot came out for the tribe of Asher, clan by clan. Their territory included: …Abdon, Rehob, Hammon and** Kanah, **as far as Greater Sidon… These towns and their villages were the inheritance of the tribe of Asher, clan by clan.** (Underline added for emphasis.)

Jesus went to Cana in Galilee, not the Kanah that belonged to the tribe of Asher. What would be the significance if Jesus had entered Kanah? In the Bible, God prophesied the future for the tribe of Asher.

Genesis 49:20 reads: **Asher's food will be rich; he will provide delicacies fit for a king.**

"Kanah" looks similar to "Cana." Yet each is distinctive in location and spiritual significance. If Jesus had entered

Kanah, He would have been with the tribe prophesied as serving delicacies to a king. The placement of the first miracle in Cana in Galilee as compared to Kanah is consistent with God's purpose: This was not the right time for Asher to serve a king. Instead, in Cana, we will find the King serving the guests. So, here we see Jesus entering Cana and, instead of being served delicacies, He is informed by his mother in John 2:3b, **"They have no more wine."**

When details in your life line up a certain way, don't jump to the conclusion that you know what God is doing. Sometimes, in our eagerness to act, we start connecting the dots for God. We start to anticipate and finish God's sentences. But there are times when facts may look one way, but life isn't what it appears to be. God wants to decide the time He will forward His purpose, and He will decide the way He will do so.

John 2:4a reads: **"Dear woman, why do you involve me?" Jesus replied.**

Answering Mary's statement about the shortage of wine, Jesus sounds annoyed. However, if this was God's season for Jesus to be a servant to the people, why would Jesus be annoyed? I submit to you that Jesus wasn't annoyed. To better understand His response, we must first understand what Mary was asking. So, let's explore that question more closely.

Jesus addressed his mother by the term "woman." The first woman in the Bible was Eve, in the Garden of Eden. The first man, Adam, followed Eve by eating the apple God commanded them not to eat. Jesus is the second and greater Adam who God sent into the world to succeed in obedience where the first Adam failed. Herein is the dramatic tension.

Will Jesus, the new Adam, follow the request of the woman in his life in a way that is outside of God's timing and will?

According to Wesley's personal notes in *Bible Study Tools,* Jesus' words, "Woman, why do you involve me?" carried a sentiment that meant "your business and my business are separate and we have nothing to do with each other." Jesus wasn't expressing annoyance but clarifying roles. The words "Why do you involve me?" carry the same meaning as expressed in 2 Kings 3:13a, which reads: Elisha said to the king of Israel, "What do we have to do with each other? Go to the prophets of your father and the prophets of your mother."

"Why do you involve me?" carries the same meaning as Ezra 4:3, which reads, "...You have no part with us in building a temple to our God..."

Jesus was telling Mary that she wasn't God, and that there are decisions only God the Father, the Son, and the Spirit will make. Have you ever tried to make decisions for God and tried to take over His world?

John 2:4b reads: **Jesus replied, "My time has not yet come."**

What was Mary really asking Jesus to do? Was it just to provide wine to party guests who had run out? What Mary was asking was revealed by Jesus' words, "My time has not yet come."

Wesley's personal notes in *Bible Study Tools* said that Jesus' response tells us that "Mary's request had in it more than a desire for the gift of wine. What she principally wanted was to have Jesus manifest himself as Messiah."

Three decades ago, the angel had appeared to Mary at a time when she was pledged to be wed to Joseph. She was told that God had chosen her for a virgin birth. Luke 1:34–35 recorded the story: **"How will this be," Mary asked the angel, "since I am a virgin?" The angel answered, "The Holy Spirit will come upon you, and the power of the Most High will overshadow you. So the holy one to be born will be called the Son of God."**

After Jesus was born, God confirmed Mary's child as the Messiah. Luke Chapter 2 tells of how a heavenly host of angels appeared in the sky to praise God for sending a Savior to the world. The shepherds in the field witnessed the heavenly choir and told Mary and Joseph of the marvelous sight. If you've ever shared with a friend the fantastic fireworks of a July 4th celebration, just imagine the excitement of the shepherds as they talked about the sky lighting up with God's heavenly host. Besides telling Mary and Joseph, the shepherds couldn't contain their excitement and spread the word on what they had seen. While those who heard the shepherds' testimony were amazed, there was no indication that the amazement lasted. However, in Mary's case, Luke 2:19 tells us, **"But Mary treasured up all these things and pondered them in her heart."**

All these years, Mary had treasured in her heart the fact that Jesus was the Messiah. We're not talking about one or two years. Imagine Jesus growing into a toddler, then an adolescent, then a teenager, then an adult. We're talking about thirty years of God's silence! Meanwhile, imagine what the neighbors were saying. Can you imagine Mary longing for God to rip open the sky and announce to the world that hers truly wasn't a pregnancy out of wedlock? Did people really believe that she was a virgin delivering God's son?

Jesus is never mistaken when it comes to our motives. He saw Mary's real appeal. She wasn't just asking Jesus to meet the need of the lack of wine. She was asking Him to show the crowds that He was the Messiah. Jesus corrected Mary because God had already chosen the sign to prove His Messiah-ship. That sign was in Jesus' death and resurrection. In John 8:28, Jesus explains this: **"When you have lifted up the Son of Man, then you will know that I am [the one I claim to be] and that I do nothing on my own but speak just what the Father has taught me."**

In Cana, Jesus had just begun His ministry, and it wasn't the time to prove His Messiah-ship. More than that, Jesus definitely wasn't going to prove His Messiah-ship with a sign that was different than the one God had picked. While Jesus did end up turning the water into wine, He did it quietly.

Have you ever rushed God because His intervention served your personal purpose? Perhaps you've been telling everyone about God's power and you don't want to be embarrassed. When you asked God for a miracle, was it because you wanted the world to see God's power? Or was it because you wanted to look spiritual in front of others by flaunting how God came through for you?

MY APPLICATION

God's timing isn't random. It fits into His overall plan for the world. The more I study God's Word, the more I'm able to discern His timing. In the distinction of Cana of Galilee versus Kanah of the Old Testament, God showed me that the two words, though similar, were totally different places. Moreover, each had its own history and spiritual significance. Outward appearances have a way of deceiving us. I must be careful not to jump to conclusions over what God is doing. Even if the signs seem to be pointing to a certain future, I need to let God reveal it in His time.

When I look at my life, I can identify times when I tried to finish God's sentences. For example, when a door opened for a job, I immediately assumed this was my opportunity. Then, when someone else was given the position, I felt cheated of my big chance. In reality, the open door was never mine. Instead of jumping ahead of God and getting disappointed, I need to trust His timing. If there is a blessing God wants for me, then no one will be able to keep me from it. God is perfectly able to fulfill His purpose for me at a time that fits into His overall plans.

There are some decisions reserved for the Godhead to make. As much as Jesus respected his mother, Mary, there are some decisions where she had no say in the matter. I wonder if I've ever tried to force my way in an area that wasn't my business. When I was working in a major management consulting company, I remember the partner telling me to smoke a cigar. I asked myself, "Why did he say that? What in the world did he mean?" Then he explained that there are times in meetings where the best thing to do is to get acclimated with what is going on before saying anything. He said, "The good thing about men smoking cigars is because taking a puff forces you to pause." It was his way to teach me to slow down and stop rushing in to offer solutions in areas I wasn't familiar with. I learned to breathe in, breathe out, and to stop stepping on toes in my zeal to be helpful.

God cannot be manipulated to act sooner than He planned. God had already decided that the ultimate sign of Jesus' Messiah-ship would be through the resurrection, and an opportunity to spectacularly change water into wine at a wedding in Cana couldn't change that. In ministry, have I ever pushed God into a personal deadline? I must admit there have been times I wanted to jettison the people involved with a ministry or project and asked God to finish His own mission. I've even asked God to throw me out and appoint someone else. God had to remind me that the goal is never a building or a program; the goal is my heart and hearts of the people. God wants a holy people who will adjust their priorities for Him. One way God tests my heart is to allow delays in a project. Then He gets to see if I worship Him or a deadline.

YOUR APPLICATION

Describe a time you connected the dots incorrectly and wrongly concluded God's purpose or timing for your family, your company, or ministry. What can you do to be sure it's God's timing and not your own ambition?

DAY 1

WHEN GOD SEPARATES US TO

WITNESS A MIRACLE, WE ARE IN

TRAINING—ARE YOU PART OF

GOD'S CUSTOMIZED LEADERSHIP

TRAINING PROGRAM?

—————

THE APOSTLE JOHN MADE THE SPECIFIC POINT IN JOHN 2:1b that **"Jesus' mother was there."** Nelson's Illustrated Bible Dictionary said, "Among the Jewish people a wedding was a festive occasion in which the whole community participated..." Compared to the guests who joined the celebration as part of a community occasion, Mary was "there," suggesting she was expected to be there. Perhaps this was her network and social circle.

In contrast to Mary being "there," the Apostle John also said in John 2:2 **"and Jesus and his disciples had also**

been invited to the wedding." Jesus was Mary's son and so He was invited. The disciples were invited because of their association with Jesus. They were like the tag-a-longs. Think of a family where the kids come home for Spring Break and get to go to a party because the head of the family was invited. Not only do the kids get to go, but the friends the kids brought home get to go as well.

Have you ever felt like you were a tag-a-long following someone around with no clear purpose of your contribution at an event? Know that if you are in God's will or walking with a godly leader, you are never an extra. You are in a planned relationship with a planned purpose. The disciples were present because their presence fit into God's plans. God intended to make them witnesses of Jesus' first miracle because this was part of their development as future leaders.

John 2:8b-10 tells us: **They did so, and the master of the banquet tasted the water that had been turned into wine. He did not realize where it had come from, though the servants who had drawn the water knew. Then he called the bridegroom aside and said, "Everyone brings out the choice wine first and then the cheaper wine after the guests have had too much to drink; but you have saved the best till now."**

After Jesus turned the water into wine, He instructed the servants to draw some out and take it to the master of the banquet. He didn't tell the servants to pass the wine out to the crowds. The master of the banquet was singled out to taste the wine. By tasting the wine and assessing it as a fine wine, the Apostle John uses the master of the banquet as the first witness to the miracle.

The fact that the bridegroom was also made aware of the quality of the wine implied he then tasted it. He, therefore, was the second witness. As I mentioned before, in the Jewish culture, the testimony of two witnesses proves a fact. God wanted to be sure we knew that Jesus turned water into wine.

Why was it important for us to know this?

Exodus 7:19 reads: **The LORD said to Moses, "Tell Aaron, 'Take your staff and stretch out your hand over the waters of Egypt—over the streams and canals, over the ponds and all the reservoirs'—and they will turn to blood. Blood will be everywhere in Egypt, even in the wooden buckets and stone jars."**

Observe that God used Moses to turn the water into blood. Years ago, when Moses was on earth, the same stone jars were filled with blood. In contrast, Jesus filled the stone jars with wine. The people expected that when the Messiah came, he would be greater than Moses. So, here God shows us that Jesus is the Messiah, the greater Moses, by turning water into wine.

What evidence has God given you to prove His existence? Was there a prayer that He answered? Was there a revelation you received from His Word? Was there a situation where you were sure God intervened to save you? When God gives us evidence, either through His Word or actions, we are responsible for remembering it.

Since John 2:9 tells us that the master of the banquet **"did not realize where it had come from, though the servants who had drawn the water knew,"** we know the servants didn't disclose to the master of the banquet that

Jesus was the one who turned the water into wine. Since neither the master of the banquet nor the bridegroom knew where the wine came from, the people enjoyed the wine without realizing it was miraculously produced. Who, then, did God perform the miracle for? John 2:11 tells us, **"He thus revealed his glory, and his disciples put their faith in him."**

Though God desires to reach the masses, He often works through individuals. He chose to reserve the first miracle mainly for His disciples. God is always interested in developing the leadership of His inner circle. In reaching the world, did you overlook developing those near you? Did you know that you can reach more people by developing the faith of those around you?

My application

When God placed the disciples in proximity to Jesus and His activities, the proximity was for a purpose. God doesn't randomly weave us into the life of a great leader. I still recall what I learned while serving as a leader in Beth Moore's class. She showed up to teach even when her heart was breaking. She taught me about leading with a broken heart.

Years after I left Beth's class, God opened the door for me to be in the inn0er circle of a ministry's top leaders. There were times I was unsure of my role at meetings. Was

I supposed to say something or just observe? Then, one day, I was given my own assignment. I was surprised over how much I had absorbed. Without intending to, I had learned some practical skills to manage a ministry.

When God gave me a mentor, I was granted private and personal time. The proximity allowed the values of my mentor to be transferred to me. When there was a shortage in resources, I found myself instinctively redirecting resources from myself to assist the staff. I told the staff, "There are so many things I can't control, but one thing I can control is my own preferences." Because I had close proximity to a mentor who was selfless, I was taught servant leadership. The longer I live, the more I am amazed at how strategic God is in placing us in the right circles. So, today I don't take my networks for granted. Instead, I ask, "What does God want me to learn?"

YOUR APPLICATION

Describe a time you witnessed something miraculous. How has your proximity to God's miraculous intervention prepared you for what God then led you to do? If you hesitate to accept God's invitation, thinking you are unprepared, please, think again! Could it be that your background was intentionally crafted for a moment such as this?

DAY 2

WHEN GOD IS READY TO ACT,

CHOOSE THE LEVEL OF YOUR

BLESSINGS—DON'T LIMIT

YOUR BLESSINGS BY YOUR

PARTIAL OBEDIENCE.

I N JOHN 2:3B, WHEN JESUS' MOTHER SAID TO HIM, **"They have no more wine,"** the situation was one of total depletion. What resource are you running out of? When there is no more hope, no more strength, no more resources, the scene is set for God to intervene.

If God hasn't intervened yet, could it be because you are still depending on what you have left? As long as there is still some more, you haven't arrived at a "no more" situation. John 2:7 reads: **Jesus said to the servants, "Fill the jars with water;" so they filled them to the brim.**

It was only when the jars were completely depleted that God created the opportunity for the jars to be filled with water "to the brim." If the jars hadn't been completed depleted, the servants would've been limited in what they could've poured in. Has it ever occurred to you that God allows total depletion to create the opportunity for total involvement? You don't get to add to what is there. You get to start from nothing and build it up.

When the servants followed Jesus' instruction, they could have filled the jars halfway. Jesus didn't tell them to fill the jars to the brim. However, because they filled the jars to the brim, when Jesus turned the water to wine, there was more wine than if the jars had been partially filled. Could it be that sometimes God won't instruct us specifically because He is giving us a choice? Our greater surrender leads to greater blessing, but God will give us the choice as to how much blessing we want.

When you hear a command from God, do you obey it to the fullest or are you a halfway person? Did you know that the more you obey, the more you give God room to bless you? Are you limiting your blessings by your partial obedience?

MY APPLICATION

God is always on time. It was at the moment when there was no more wine that God stepped in to solve the problem. When I get anxious during the times God delays, perhaps I'm the one causing the delay. Perhaps God is waiting for me to exhaust my self-effort before He will intervene. I have a tendency to try to figure everything out. What I need to do is begin in a place of total depletion by going to God in humility and asking for His help. I need to say, "Father, give me your ideas. Show me the answer so I can solve the problem according to your wisdom." My human flesh gets nervous when I think of getting to the end of my resources. What I learned from the words "they have no more" is that the point of "no more" is the turning point for God to step in.

God's power in our lives is released in proportion to the level of our obedience. Is my lack of obedience limiting my blessings? I remember taking my dog to obedience school. When I went to pick him up, the instructor said, "You have an 80% dog." What was an 80% dog? He said, "Your dog obeys 80% of the time." The instructor wanted to manage my expectations so I wouldn't be disappointed by my dog's partial obedience. If I say "sit" or "heel," I could expect the dog to obey eight-out-of-ten times. I asked the instructor why the dog was an 80% dog. He said, "Because he wants to be." He then said that some dogs are just that way. My dog would never make it in the police force or in a noble role of a seeing-eye dog. He would be too unpredictable. My 80% canine made me think about my life. Am I missing out on being chosen for a noble role because God sees me as unpredictable? Can God trust me to be 100% obedient?

YOUR APPLICATION

Describe a time when you gave God a token of obedience instead of obeying 100%. How do you think your partial obedience caused you to miss out on maximum blessings?

Day 3
Devotion

AT THE CROSSROADS OF

LIFE, GOD GIVES US HIS

INSTRUCTION—OUR CHOICES

IN KEY MOMENTS WILL

ESTABLISH OUR LEGACY.

W HEN JESUS TOLD MARY HIS TIME HAD NOT COME TO display the sign of His Messiah-ship, she immediately backed away and said to the servants in John 2:5, **"Do whatever he tells you."** In Mary's response, we have a stark contrast to what happened in the Garden of Eden with the first woman, Eve.

In the Book of Genesis, God created Adam and Eve to have authority on earth. They were to exert authority over the animals and the plants. What God required of them was not to eat the fruit of one tree. Their ability to overcome the apple tree, i.e., a plant, would keep God's original chain of authority. According to Dr. Charles Baylis' lectures at Dallas Theological Seminary, God's original chain of command was God over humankind over animal over plants. This order was turned upside down when Adam and Eve ate the apple, thereby letting the plant overcome humankind.

Eve was deceived by the Devil into thinking that God was withholding something good from her. In Genesis 3:4–5, the Devil said to Eve, **"You will not surely die …For God knows that when you eat of it your eyes will be opened, and you will be like God, knowing good and evil."** Don't miss the subtlety of the Devil's deception. Here he was enticing Eve with being **"like God."** Meanwhile Genesis 1:27 tells us, **"So God created man in his own image, in the image of God he created him; male and female he created them."** If Eve was already made in God's image, then what else was missing that would make her like God? Do you see how the Devil always wants us to think that God is withholding something from us? He wants us to be dissatisfied and to doubt God's goodness.

Fast forward to where we hear Jesus' mother telling her son, "They have no more wine." We then see Jesus, the new Adam, pitted against the grape plant. For Jesus to maintain authority over the plant, He couldn't defy God's purpose and timing in response to the wine shortage. The wine shortage couldn't rush God to perform a grand display of Jesus' Messiah-ship. Whatever Jesus chose to do, He had to do it in a way consistent with the extent God wanted Him to reveal His Messiah-ship at that time of His ministry. Jesus responded to the need discreetly.

Mary showed herself different from Eve by the way she submitted to Jesus. She, unlike Eve who persuaded Adam, didn't try to persuade the new Adam. She didn't pressure, she didn't manipulate. Instead, she chose to trust in God's timing. She backed away and said in John 2:5b, **"Do whatever he tells you."**

Eve chose to doubt God's goodness. Mary chose to trust God's timing. Eve disobeyed God. Mary chose to submit to God's instructions. No matter your background, will you be the one to change your legacy into one of obedience to God instead of rebellion to His purpose?

My application

God gives each person a chance to make his or her own decision. Just because Eve disobeyed didn't mean Mary had to disobey. The sin of one generation does not necessarily pass down to the next. In my life, my mother lost faith in God and took her own life. When I face challenges, there are times I find myself thinking, "If my mother's choice was good enough for my mother, it's good enough for me!" Mary's story reminds me that I am not stuck in a generational sin. I have the opportunity to break any negative patterns and to change my family's legacy. Will I continue a legacy of faithlessness or will I endure in faith and establish a legacy of victory? The choice is mine. God gave me free will so I could choose Him over evil.

YOUR APPLICATION

Describe a problem you inherited from a previous leader or someone whose wrong decisions created consequences that were passed down to you. How does knowing you can establish your own legacy help you to solve the problem? What legacy will you leave?

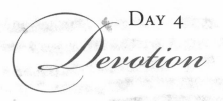

DAY 4

GOD USHERS IN TIMES OF

JUDGMENT AS WELL AS TIMES

OF BLESSING—DON'T KEEP

PUNISHING YOURSELF WHEN YOU

ARE IN A SEASON OF BLESSING.

A FTER CORRECTING MARY'S MOTIVE, JESUS RESPONDED to the wine shortage, but for a different motive. He wasn't demonstrating the ultimate sign of his Messiah-ship in a grand display. Instead, He changed water into wine for the disciples to witness as part of their training program. John 2:6 tells us, **Nearby stood six stone water jars, the kind used by the Jews for ceremonial washing, each holding from twenty to thirty gallons.** The words "stone jars" appeared in the Old Testament when Moses turned water into blood. Exodus 7:19 tells us: **The LORD said** to Moses, "Tell Aaron, 'Take your staff and stretch out your hand over the waters of Egypt—over the streams and canals, over the ponds and all the reservoirs'—and they will turn to blood. Blood will be everywhere in Egypt, even in the wooden buckets and stone jars." (Underline added for emphasis.)

In the Old Testament, Moses turned the water in the stone jars into blood as a sign of judgment. In the New Testament, Jesus turned water into wine. While the Old Testament offered the people the Law and judgment as their way to please God, the New Testament ushered in a time of grace and the gift of Jesus to cover the penalty of our sins. If you are in a season of blessing, are you the one putting yourself back in bondage?

MY APPLICATION

God operates in seasons of judgment and seasons of grace. If God is showing grace, then heaven forbid that I put myself back into a season of judgment. When in my twenties, I was consumed with the goal of finding Mr. Right. I was ready to compromise my beliefs just to be with someone. My choices led me to heartbreak after heartbreak. In utter desperation I cried out to God to rescue me. In His grace, He brought me to my prince. God ushered in a season of blessing. However, my husband would often say to me, "Why do you keep returning to the past?" Indeed, he was right. I found myself recycling through past mistakes and resurrecting old memories of rejection. God wanted me to live in a season of blessing, but I was the one who kept myself in a season of judgment for my past mistakes. I had to learn to discern my seasons and to celebrate the blessings. I had to examine reality and ask myself, "Is this really a season of hardship? Or is this a season of blessing that the Devil is trying to confuse me into thinking is one of judgment?"

Your application

Describe a time you kept dwelling on past mistakes. How did you keep yourself under judgment instead of celebrating God's blessings?

DAY 5

DISCERN GOD'S "NOW" MOMENT

OF A COMPLETED MIRACLE—

WHEN GOD SAYS "NOW," DON'T

MISS THE GREEN LIGHT TO

RECEIVE YOUR BLESSING.

IN JOHN 2:8, JESUS TOLD THE SERVANTS, **"Now draw some out and take it to the master of the banquet."** "Now" pinpoints a specific moment in time. In Wesley's explanatory notes in *Bible Study Tools*, he said, "The word now seems to indicate the turning-point when the water became wine."

After Jesus stated a "Now" moment, and the water had been turned into wine, He instructed the servants in John 2:8 to **"draw some out and take it to the master of the banquet."** Immediately after Jesus stated the "Now" moment, the next step was to invite the servants to "draw" out the wine and enjoy the blessing.

When God says, "Now, rise up!" do you say, "No, not yet!"? When God says, "Now, you are healed!" do you say, "Are you sure?" When God says, "Now, go!" do you say, "I'm not ready yet!"?

There was an exact point in time when the water had completely turned into wine. There was no reason to delay serving the wine, especially when the guests were still present and Mary had already stated in John 2:3 **"They have no more wine."** When the need is clear and present, God is ready to meet it when He says "The transformation is complete. The time to receive the blessing is 'Now'!" Any further delay in receiving the blessing is a lack of faith.

My application

There is a definite moment in time when God is ready to release His power. I can remember the day I had an "Aha!" moment that changed my life. It was an exact moment when God's truth set me free. I was beating myself up for not being more sensitive to my mother's depression. I blamed myself for failing to rescue her. I wanted so much to relive the past and to undo some actions, but with my mother's death, I knew I no longer had the opportunity to respond differently. Then, one day, I heard God say, "That's why Jesus had to come." In that exact moment, I realized that no matter how hard we try, fallen humanity will always mess up in some way. But, oh, the grace of God to send Jesus to pay the penalty of all our sins, whether deliberate or accidental! Jesus paid it all, and God wanted me to know the miracle is complete. There was not one more thing I could add to what Jesus did for me on the cross. With Jesus' death for me, God wiped the slate clean. The blood of Jesus washed me white as snow. Once God spoke His truth into my heart, the "Now" moment for my healing was completed. The next step was for me to enjoy the blessing.

YOUR APPLICATION

Describe a time when you could mark the moment a truth from God's Word transformed your life. How have you remained in the freedom of that truth?

Weekend Reflection

My application

In fulfilling God's marching order to establish Inspire Women, I wanted God to perform a miracle so I could be done with building the pillars of the ministry. I was never aggravated by the setbacks before, but with the loss of my spiritual father and the declining health of my spiritual mother, I felt a deep sense of loneliness. Every challenge I faced felt harder without them. Every success I experienced reminded me of their absence to celebrate with me. I wanted to escape, perhaps find a change of scenery or move to a different city. I didn't want to be reminded daily that the ones who were at the beginning of the dream wouldn't witness its fulfillment.

God had to remind me it was important to Him to include others in building the pillars. This might involve delays because not everyone is in tune with God's purpose. In God's mercy, He wanted to wait for others to get on the same page. His priority wasn't to hurry in order to lessen my pain. Life wasn't about me! Will I love the people enough to endure the delays? Will I labor tirelessly to help as many as possible to be part of God's story?

Your application

Describe a current delay in life that aggravates you. Is it finding the right medication? Is it getting the needed resource for a business? Is it the preparation time it takes to equip you for a future dream? Say why the delay aggravated you. Then state how God is using the delay to refine your character and to give you greater clarity in your priorities and purpose in life.

4

Release plans that no longer work

"Giving up doesn't always mean you are weak ...sometimes it means that you are strong enough to let go."

~ Anonymous

TODAY'S CHAPTER INTRODUCES US to a man with a consuming question: "*Where am I heading?*" Can anyone relate? He may be further along than some of us in that he knew where he wanted to go. He had a plan, a system to get there. He just wanted to know, "Will what I am doing get me there?" Do you have a question like that? Have you ever had that dreadful sense that what you counted on to get you to your destination might not be enough?

The Apostle John tells us about Nicodemus, a leader who showed up on the scene, wrestling with a question about eternal life. Imagine being sure of a direction, only to realize your current path won't get you to your destination. Some people know they are at a dead end but are unwilling to change direction. They stay stuck in what isn't working while hoping for the best. Perhaps they invested too much time and find it too painful to admit they have wasted years on the wrong path. Others might immediately cut their losses and start looking for a different path. Then there are those who know their current path isn't working but don't know what else to do. As they try to figure out an answer, they long for someone to come along who could offer them a solution. Do you long for such a friend in your life?

When I first went to college, I couldn't figure out what to major in. A friend who had my best interest at heart informed me that I didn't have the luxury to figure out what I wanted to do with my life. The counsel I received was, "Just pick the field where you can be guaranteed a job!" As I look back at that time, I recall that most of the incoming freshmen weren't sure where they were heading. Yet there were a few who always knew what they wanted to do with their lives. They had a sure plan to get where they wanted to go in life. However, when they graduated, something changed in the economy. Their sure path to the job of their dreams resulted in their standing in the unemployment line. They were more devastated than the ones who were less sure of life!

Are you among those who actually knew what you wanted in life? However, maybe you're no longer sure of how to reach your dreams. Perhaps the rules have changed. Perhaps the opportunities have changed. Perhaps the people in your life have changed. All you know is the plan you were sure of yesterday won't work today. The question is, when you are working with a wrong plan, will you have the courage to give it up? Nicodemus was in such a place where he discovered he was working with the wrong plan to get to heaven. In his panic, he reached out for help.

John 3:1–2 reads: **Now there was a man of the Pharisees named Nicodemus, a member of the Jewish ruling council. He came to Jesus at night and said, "Rabbi, we know you are a teacher who has come from God. For no one could perform the miraculous signs you are doing if God were not with him."**

Nicodemus, a ruler among the Pharisees, was drawn to Jesus and went to see him at night. He didn't apologize for intruding on Jesus' evening hours. Have you noticed that those who have power or influence often don't ask permission to change your schedule? They are used to having people reschedule their lives to meet their needs. But here we have the dramatic tension of Nicodemus, a leader of the Jewish ruling class, meeting with Jesus, the God of the Universe. Which leader will defer to the other? We see Jesus, the greater leader, humbly serving Nicodemus by letting him intrude on his time in the middle of the night.

Since he was a leader, we can expect Nicodemus to be more discerning. We then see that, in his discernment, he decided to seek Jesus out. We are told that He picked Jesus after concluding in John 3:2b that Jesus wouldn't be performing miracles **"if God were not with him."** How did

Nicodemus know that God was with Jesus? Nicodemus made his assessment based on watching Jesus "perform the miraculous signs."

When we are confused, we don't need to be talking to other people who are confused. What we need is to find someone whose life evidences success. Who are you talking to about your life? Who are you listening to for advice? What tangible evidence do you see in the people you're speaking to that proves their credibility and wisdom?

I remember sharing with my husband someone's advice in raising children. I thought the counsel was sound and impressive. My husband had this very baffled look on his face. "What's wrong?" I asked. He said, "I don't think this person you are so impressed with is doing that well with her children." Oh my, why didn't I put two and two together? Why was I taking parental advice from somebody who wasn't doing well in her own family? I then realized that I was impressed with the talk when I needed to look for tangible results. Nicodemus' story reminded me that we need to look for help from someone who is proven in their area of expertise. Let what they have done be their resume, not what they say.

I recall a time when I was struggling with a gas leak in the house. I couldn't figure out where the odor was coming from. When I called the gas company, they sent a technician to assess the situation. When he came into the house, he knew exactly what to look for and where to look for it. The fact is, when someone is a master of their field, they can zero in on the answer quickly. They seldom need you to elaborate on the details because they've heard the question phrased many times and various ways. They have an experience base where they know what the issue is without your long explanation.

When my sons were preschoolers, I was frequently calling the pediatrician for one thing or another. Usually, as I was explaining the symptoms, it took but one or two key words for the doctor to know what was going on. In the same way, we see Nicodemus going to Jesus with a pressing question about eternal life. Perhaps it was the look on his face that was the giveaway. Perhaps it was the fact that he was a leader of the Pharisees and coming to Jesus secretly at night. Jesus, being God, was a master when it came to questions about God. Jesus answered Nicodemus' question before he asked it.

John 3:3 tells us: **In reply Jesus declared, "I tell you the truth, no one can see the kingdom of God unless he is born again."**

John 3:3a begins with the words **"In reply Jesus declared..."** In reply to what? Nicodemus didn't ask a question. He made two statements in John 3:2. First he said, **"Rabbi, we know you are a teacher who has come from God."** Then he said, **"For no one could perform the miraculous signs you are doing if God were not with him."** In his two statements, Nicodemus didn't directly ask Jesus a question. Normally when we make statements to someone about themselves, the response we get back is "Thank you" or "You're right to observe that" or "No, that's not exactly what I stand for." We don't usually get an answer to a question we didn't ask.

The question Nicodemus didn't verbalize concerned how to get into the Kingdom of God. Jesus knew what was bothering Nicodemus and answered the unspoken question.

Jesus said in John 3:3, **"I tell you the truth, no one can see the kingdom of God unless he is born again."**

If you've wrestled with a question for so long you can't even put your worry into words, here's the good news. Jesus has the answer when life has gotten so complicated that you aren't even sure what the question is anymore. Jesus has the answer when the plan you counted on isn't working anymore. Jesus has the answer for questions as serious as eternal life and everything else.

God is all-knowing and He knows our questions before we express them. In my life, when I ask God, "What's wrong with me?" I often never wait for an answer. Instead, I rush down the path of trying to figure it out myself. What am I feeling? What is the cause of my lack of peace? Why am I sad? The questions are endless. There are times I confuse myself with my questions that are shooting off in every direction. It is during these times that I will crawl into my bed and put the covers over my head. I have to force myself to get quiet and to stop asking questions. I have to simply say, "God I don't know what's wrong, please help me." And then I let myself fall asleep and expect God to refresh my mind and give me His answers the next morning. When I wake up, it's like He starts to download the answer. When I finally clear my own mind, I start to hear Him clearly.

Psalms 46:10 says: **Be still, and know that I am God; I will be exalted among the nations, I will be exalted in the earth.**

Perhaps you are weary of asking questions that offer no final answer. Are you tired of answers that say, "It could be this" or "It could be that?" To get away from the question, did you go on vacation, go shopping, or throw yourself into a project while leaving the question unanswered?

Nicodemus wanted to settle the answer to eternal life, once and for all. He hung on to every word from Jesus' mouth. However, he interpreted information based on what he was used to. He came from his own familiar context. As a Pharisee, Nicodemus was a teacher of the Law and well-versed in all the requirements of the law. As one who followed the Law, he depended on his own discipline and behavior. He automatically interpreted the instruction from Jesus in **John 3:3b** to be **"born again"** as something he could do. What Nicodemus wanted were the steps.

John 3:4 reads: **"How can a man be born when he is old?" Nicodemus asked. "Surely he cannot enter a second time into his mother's womb to be born!"**

Have you always counted on a task list to get to your goal? If you're someone who finds security in a task list, you may be experiencing anxiety when the goal is too big for one. In the question for eternal life, God wanted Nicodemus to see that he couldn't depend on himself. There are some destinations no human can reach on his or her own. Some destinations are so grand that only God can make a way. Such is the destination of eternal life.

John 3:5–7 reads: **Jesus answered, "I tell you the truth, no one can enter the kingdom of God unless he is born of water and the Spirit. Flesh gives birth to flesh, but the Spirit gives birth to spirit. You should not be surprised at my saying, 'You must be born again.'"**

In **John 3:5b**, while Nicodemus was depending on his human effort to enter the Kingdom of God, Jesus redirected him to a new birth "of water and the Spirit." Jesus was telling Nicodemus that what God wanted wasn't only our physical birth through the water of the birth canal, but also a birth of the Spirit. In order to enter heaven, human flesh could not attain the level of holiness or perfection that met God's standards. In order to enter heaven, it took trusting in the work of the Spirit.

Jesus then drew on the metaphor of wind from the Old Testament to describe the Spirit. Therefore, Jesus said in John 3:8, **"The wind blows wherever it pleases. You hear its sound, but you cannot tell where it comes from or where it is going. So it is with everyone born of the Spirit."** He was referring to life as breathed into us through God's Spirit.

The idea of wind in the Old Testament was always connected with the activity of the Spirit and new life. Ezekiel 37:3–10 reads: **He asked me, "Son of man, can these bones live?" I said, "O Sovereign LORD, you alone know." ..."I will make breath enter you, and you will come to life...Then you will know that I am the LORD."...Then he said to me, "Prophesy to the breath; prophesy, son of man, and say to it, 'This is what the Sovereign LORD says: Come from the four winds, O breath, and breathe into these slain, that they may live.'" So I prophesied as he commanded me, and breath entered them; they came to life and stood up on their feet—a vast army.**

When Jesus described the Spirit as a wind, He showed us the Spirit is a force no human can put in a box or control. To follow a Spirit who is described as flowing in and out of situations like the wind is a frightening idea for those who need control. The only way to relieve our anxiety over our loss of control is to increase our trust in God's Spirit. The only way to increase trust is to develop our relationship with God. The more we get to know God, the more we will trust Him.

If you are in a place with questions that only God can answer, know that His answer might take you outside the box of your familiar ideas. God will not apologize for taking you beyond your comfort zone. If you find the courage to knock on God's door, know that whatever the hour, God will meet you. He wants to answer your questions. He wants you to have both eternal life and a victorious life while on earth.

MY APPLICATION

Nicodemus was a teacher of the Law. God sent Jesus into the world to show us the Law had failed in getting fallen humanity into heaven. So, Jesus became the perfect fulfillment of the Law. He would be the unblemished lamb who would pay the full penalty of the Law for our sins. The Apostle John picked the meeting of Nicodemus with Jesus to help us understand the message that grace has entered the world to replace Law. It, therefore, fit God's purpose for Jesus to speak to a teacher of the Law.

In my life, has God ever set life up where law is confronted by grace? I recall a time when someone owed me money for rent. Because of an illness, she could not pay her rent. The law allowed me to evict her and to demand payment. However, grace led me to forgive the debt.

The description of the Spirit as a wind that blows freely is a stark contrast to seeing God as the LAW. The former puts me in an atmosphere of freedom, the latter in a state of fear and bondage. The sad thing is bondage can also feel secure, no matter how miserable we are because it is familiar. I know women who have chosen to stay in a place of bondage because it felt safer than venturing into new territory. Whether in the plan of salvation or in a plan to fulfill God's dreams for my life, God wants me to trust in Jesus' perfection. Leaning on Jesus' power, I will please God in my service on earth while heading for life in eternity. The Law failed Nicodemus because no human could keep God's commands perfectly.

Sometimes I wonder if God allows me to fail so He can direct my attention to trusting in the power of His Son. At the end of the day, God is impressed with His Son, not the imperfection of human flesh. I think I stress myself out unnecessarily when I count on my plans. I need to ask God to give me His plans and to focus on Jesus' guidance in all my decisions. My confidence isn't in a business plan, but in the person of Jesus, who will show me the way. The Christ who offers me a foolproof plan to get to heaven can certainly provide a plan through any other challenge I have on earth!

When Inspire Women was looking to operate from a permanent location, I found myself impairing the vision by my limited knowledge of local real estate. I assumed I lived in a city, and a permanent dwelling must be a concrete office building. God led me to ask Jesus what kind of building He wanted. He impressed on my heart the words "spiritual oasis." I had no idea what a spiritual oasis looked like, especially in a city like Houston. So, I simply prayed, "God, show me one step at a time." God led me to a Realtor who happened to tell me, "I have this property. It's unusual because it's on unrestricted land. I don't know if this is anything you're interested in. It looks like a park." She didn't know I was waiting on God to show me what a spiritual oasis looked like. Today, when I drive into Inspire Women's permanent spiritual oasis, I am reminded to always trust in Jesus instead of limiting myself with a human-derived plan.

YOUR APPLICATION

Describe an undertaking you couldn't possibly do in your human effort. Perhaps you're struggling with a challenge with your children or a project at work. Share how your human attempts failed to give you the wisdom you needed to succeed. Share how your success was totally dependent on God's grace. State what this experience taught you about yourself and God's guidance.

DAY 1
Devotion

DON'T BEAT YOURSELF UP IF

YOU CAN'T FIGURE OUT THE

ANSWER—SOME ANSWERS IN

LIFE WERE MEANT FOR GOD

ALONE TO REVEAL.

A S A LEADER HIMSELF, NICODEMUS RECOGNIZED THE leadership attributes in another leader. He didn't form his assessment based on what Jesus said he would do, but on what he saw Jesus doing. He said to Jesus in John 3:2b, **"we know you are a teacher who has come from God. For no one could perform the miraculous signs you are doing if God were not with him."** The key verb is "doing."

As Nicodemus concluded that Jesus was "*a teacher,*" he either heard Jesus teach or heard others report about Jesus' teaching. We also know that Nicodemus was aware of the content of the teaching. He described Jesus in John 3:2 as "a teacher who has come from God." It seems that Jesus' teaching wasn't only in words, but it evidenced God's power. We know this because in John 3:2b, Nicodemus referred to Jesus' teaching substantiated by "the miraculous signs you are doing."

If you've ever gone to a seminar, think about what draws you to the speaker. Often, the speaker that draws the crowd has a proven resume. Often, the advertising for the speaker includes the speaker's accomplishments and recognitions. In a similar way, Nicodemus was drawn to Jesus as a teacher with proven accomplishments.

Yet don't miss Nicodemus' limitations in his assessment of Jesus. In John 3:2a, Nicodemus concluded that Jesus was a teacher "who has come from God," and that God was "with him." Nicodemus overlooked Jesus being God Himself in the flesh. Could it be that some truths will never be seen through human effort? Some truths, only God can reveal.

My Application

Our human minds cannot possibly fathom God's mind. There are some truths that we will never be able to figure out on our own. Some truths, only God can reveal. Recently, when I watched a movie on the life of Pope Paul II,

I witnessed how God answered the Pope's question on why he was suffering. In one scene in the movie, the Pope was very disturbed when he was in chronic pain after breaking his hips. He then showed signs of Parkinson's disease and couldn't understand why God allowed his illness when he had so much work to do in the church. Then, one day, God revealed to him that families and the church were suffering. The Pope then willingly accepted his suffering as his way to fellowship with the pain in the world.

In my own life, I asked God why I had to feel the pressures of the needs of those called to missions and ministry. One day, a pastor friend of mine said, "God called you to be a burden carrier." Immediately I felt God's peace. Once I settled my calling, I felt confident God would give me the strength to take care of everything on my platter. As one called to be a burden carrier, I find myself solving problems for individuals and organizations. I find myself concerned when individuals want to quit serving God or when ministries are going under. For the first time in my life, I understood the concern I had was part of my calling. The ability to respond to the need is empowered by God, and He gets all the credit.

YOUR APPLICATION

Describe a time God revealed something to you that you would never have figured out in your own power. Perhaps it was someone you shouldn't trust or a direction you needed to take with your family or with an organization. What action did you take as a result of God's revelation?

DAY 2

Devotion

GOD EXPECTS US TO MATURE

IN UNDERSTANDING HIS

PURPOSE—IF YOU ARE STILL

CONFUSED, ARE YOU STUNTING

YOUR OWN GROWTH?

———◆———

THE CONCEPT OF DEPENDING ON GOD INSTEAD OF DE-pending on himself was so foreign to Nicodemus that he said in John 3:9, **"How can this be?"** To this Jesus responded in John 3:10, **"You are Israel's teacher...and do you not understand these things?"** What were these things that Nicodemus was supposed to have understood?

Jesus reprimanded Nicodemus for not understanding more. Should you have greater understanding by now based on how long you have journeyed with God? How long have you used the excuse that you are a young believer or that you need to do more research or reading on a certain topic?

Jesus expected Nicodemus, a teacher of Israel, to understand the Old Testament. Nicodemus should've recognized the significance of Jesus' choice of words. The idea of wind connected with life was demonstrated in the first book of the Bible, when God created humankind. Genesis 2:7 reads, **"the LORD God formed the man from the dust of the ground and breathed into his nostrils the breath of life, and the man became a living being."** When God breathed into Adam's nostril, the wind of the Spirit flowed from God into Adam.

In the Old Testament, wind was connected not only with the first signs of life, but with a new renewed life. Ezekiel 36:25–27 reads: **"I will sprinkle clean water on you, and you will be clean; I will cleanse you from all your impurities and from all your idols. I will give you a new heart and put a new spirit in you; I will remove from you your heart of stone and give you a heart of flesh. And I will put my Spirit in you and move you to follow my decrees and be careful to keep my laws."**

God spoke of a time when He would put His Spirit into humankind. His Spirit is the one who will "move you to follow my decrees and be careful to keep my laws." God wants the motivation to follow Him to come from a sense of "sonship," not a mechanical checklist. It will be God's Spirit that bonds us with Him as family. Our desire to serve God will not come from a heart that is going through the motions, but a heart that wants to be just like our heavenly Father in His holiness and mercy and love for the world.

MY APPLICATION

God expects us to live out what He has revealed to us. It displeases God when we keep learning and yet never understand His truths. Jesus reprimanded Nicodemus for being a teacher all these years and not having greater understanding of God's plans. Nicodemus was stuck in a program of rituals and offering sacrifices on the altar to appease God for sin. Jesus introduced the truth of Himself as the final sacrifice. God transitioned from a program to a person.

If left to me, I think it's much easier to be spiritual by showing up in a Bible class, going to seminary, or attending religious events. All these programs are wonderful, but they defeat their purpose if they don't lead me to the person of God! The test of my spiritual maturity isn't the events I attend but what I understand about God's person and what I then do in adjusting my life and activities. Will understanding who Jesus is and what He came to earth to do take me outside the comfort zone of my programmed activities? If, indeed, Jesus is Savior and the way to eternal life, how then should I live? What message should I be sharing with those around me who do not know Him?

Lately, I have been thinking about how God puts us in neighborhoods, yet how many of my neighbors do I know? Two years ago, with much protest to God's prompting I gave my neighbor a book I wrote titled "Transforming for a Purpose". I felt silly giving her that book and never expected her to read it. The book was about allowing God to transform our loneliness, rejection, and fear. I was caught off guard when a year later, my neighbor knocked on my door. She informed me she no longer lived in the house on my street. She and her husband were divorced. They had lost everything. While unpacking, she saw my book on her bookshelf. She was not a reader but something made her pick up the book. She wanted me to know she could not put the book down and that it changed her life. She immediately went online to order copies for all her friends. She felt compelled to stop by my house to let me know what the message of the book meant to her. After she left, I pondered her words and was truly convicted over how much I resisted sharing that book with her. God showed me once again that He trusts His message to His servants. When we withhold God's message, it's like keeping a rescue line from reaching others. I know that anytime I reach out, there's a risk. The alternative is to live safe. But I don't think living safe is the way to reach the world. God wants me to get out of my comfort zone, even if it means risking rejection.

YOUR APPLICATION

Jesus expected Nicodemus to understand what He was saying because of the many years Nicodemus had studied God's Word. How many years have you studied God's Word? Share something God revealed to you about life or yourself that you are still struggling with. What is keeping you from accepting God's truth? Is it something you must give up?

142

DAY 3

GOD EXPLAINS TRUTH IN SIMPLE

TERMS—DON'T MAKE GOD'S

ANSWER TOO COMPLICATED

AND MISS THE LIGHT IN

THE DARKNESS.

———

WHEN GOD REVEALS HIS PLAN, WE MAY HEM AND HAW and say we don't understand. God doesn't buy our procrastination. He was the one who made us and He knows that when He explains the truth, the only thing blocking us from the truth is our choice not to believe.

John 3:19–21 reads: "This is the verdict: Light has come into the world, but men loved darkness instead of light because their deeds were evil. Everyone who does evil hates the light, and will not come into the light for fear that his deeds will be exposed. But whoever lives by the truth comes into the light, so that it may be seen plainly that what he has done has been done through God."

The gavel descended, and the verdict for our sins was death. It was not a verdict that could be appealed. The penalty must be paid! The penalty required not only a lifetime sentence based on earthly years, but an eternal death sentence. God chose to pay our eternal death sentence by allowing His Son to die for us.

When Jesus came, God was reversing the darkness of our death sentence. John 3:19a says, "Light has come into the world." The sad truth was, not everyone knew they needed light in their lives. And even if they knew they needed light, many preferred the darkness because they enjoyed their sins.

If you're avoiding God or keep saying you don't understand, could it be because you are hiding sin? If you hate Christian activities, is it because you are doing what John said in John 3:20, "Everyone who does evil hates the light, and will not come into the light for fear that his deeds will be exposed?"

In describing the need to be born of the Spirit, Jesus used earthly terms such as water, wind, and childbirth. He was giving Nicodemus an illustration with earthly materials. If giving an illustration with items Nicodemus was familiar with didn't bring about understanding, Jesus was telling Nicodemus in John 3:12b, "how then will you believe if I speak of heavenly things?"

Has God ever given you an earthly illustration to make His truths come alive for you? When you still reject God's truth, is it because you didn't understand or is it because you've chosen to remain ignorant?

MY APPLICATION

God is perfectly able to speak in terms I can understand. For example, when I was struggling with whether to establish Inspire Women, He showed me the image of a death certificate. In that image, I knew He was telling me that if I didn't continue building Inspire Women, I was burying a baby alive and signing a death certificate for a dream.

Years ago, my nine-month-old son was rushed to the hospital. Unbeknownst to me, he had asthma and was having an asthma attack. I brought him in to see the pediatrician thinking he had a cold. I had no idea his windpipes were constricting. The doctor ordered his immediate admission into the hospital. I was in a panic, and my son was in a panic, probably sensing my emotions. Even today, when I recall that experience, I feel the stress of the drama! He was at that stage in life when he was beginning to recognize familiar faces and exhibiting separation anxiety with strangers. The nurse had to pry his fingers open to take him from me. He kept reaching towards me, crying out, "Mama, mama!" I was sure I was going to die that very moment as my heart was wrenched in every way. I thought, "God, you are so cruel. Why did you open my heart to love this child so deeply and then allow a situation where this child could be taken from me?"

A week later, my son was back home from the hospital. He was playing on the carpet, while I was sitting beside him. I felt the peace of just sitting next to him, happy to see him playing with his blocks. The days in the hospital were like yesterday's nightmare. He didn't seem to remember, and I was trying hard to forget. As I was playing with him, I noticed the black and blue marks on his tiny hands. Then, in that moment, God impressed on my mind a vision of Calvary. In no uncertain terms, God had shown me His suffering when He allowed the hands and feet of His Son to be bruised. Instead of feeling sorry for myself, I started to praise God for loving the world so much that He sent Jesus to die for us.

Over the years, I have learned that if we stay confused after God shows us truth so clearly, it isn't because God is unclear. It's because we choose to make God complicated.

Your application

Describe a time when God revealed His truth to you through a movie or a story someone shared with you. How did your view of life or behavior change based on what God showed you? If you haven't made any changes, state why not.

Day 4
Devotion

DON'T BLAME GOD FOR

DELAYS IN REACHING YOUR

DESTINATION—IS YOUR LACK OF

FAITH KEEPING YOU IN A DESERT?

⬩━⬩

OHN 3:14–15 READS: **Just as Moses lifted up the snake in the desert, so the Son of Man must be lifted up, that everyone who believes in him may have eternal life.**

To show Nicodemus who He was, Jesus referred to a familiar Old Testament character. In John 3:14, Jesus referenced Moses in the story about the "snake in the desert." In John 3:15, we are told that Moses lifted up the snake so that everyone who looked at it was healed from their snake bites. The story Jesus was referring to was in Numbers 21:4–9.

Numbers 21:4–9 reads: **But the people grew impatient on the way; they spoke against God and against Moses, and said, "Why have you brought us up out of**

Egypt to die in the desert? There is no bread! There is no water! And we detest this miserable food!" Then the LORD sent venomous snakes among them; they bit the people and many Israelites died. The people came to Moses and said, "We sinned when we spoke against the LORD and against you. Pray that the LORD will take the snakes away from us." So Moses prayed for the people. The LORD said to Moses, "Make a snake and put it up on a pole; anyone who is bitten can look at it and live." So Moses made a bronze snake and put it up on a pole. Then when anyone was bitten by a snake and looked at the bronze snake, he lived.

This Old Testament story tells us about the people blaming God for the delay in reaching their destination. They grew impatient and were complaining against God! Have you ever complained against God because the journey is taking longer than you expected? Are you telling God the delay is His fault?

In response to the complaints, God sent venomous snakes to bite them. Talk about a delay! It was as if God was saying, "If you really want to know what the delay is, the problem is not with me, the problem is with you!" The poison in their own heart was then made blatant by the venom from the snakes! God wasn't the bottleneck. The delay was caused by the people's lack of faith.

God then instructed Moses to make a bronze snake, to lift it up, and ask the people to look at it. Those who looked at the bronze snake were healed. There was no human logic to why looking at a bronze snake would bring healing. What God was asking for was faith. The path to healing was not by human effort but by the people obeying God's instructions. Jesus was telling Nicodemus that, in a similar way, the people in the New Testament will be healed of their sins when they look to Jesus when God lifts Him up on the cross. Are you in a wilderness today because of your lack of faith? Is it time to believe God and stop causing your own delays?

My application

God is never late. When there's a delay, I need to ask if I'm the bottleneck. Have I ever blamed God for delaying when the delay is really my fault? I can remember a time when I kept waiting for God to deliver me 9when deliverance meant I needed to be obedient. I didn't have the courage to boldly ask for help. I was fearful of rejection. It was so much easier to wait for God to do something than to pick up the phone or to make an appointment to see someone who had the means to help me.

Over the years, I learned that God chooses how He works through each person. Some people get to pray and the provision just shows up. Some people get to knock on doors and risk rejection. I believe what God wants is the path that requires greater faith. For some people who have the influence, it may be that one word from their mouth and the need will be provided. So, God forbids them to open their mouth to others and instructs them to appeal to Him only. For me, it's much harder to open my mouth to others than to pray to God. So, God opens the doors for me to see the CEO of a company or a person with the influence to help me. I go trembling, always praying that God will make the appeal for me. But sure enough, God waits for me to have the faith to ask. When I experience delay, I always begin by asking if there's something I have failed to do. Am I the bottleneck?

Your application

Describe a time your disobedience delayed the completion of God's mission. Is there something you need to do so you are no longer the cause of delay? How has your lack of faith caused a whole family or community to lose a blessing?

DAY 5

Devotion

GOD IS OFFENDED WHEN WE

REJECT JESUS AS HIS PLAN—IS

PRIDE KEEPING YOU FROM GOD'S

100% GUARANTEED PLAN?

JOHN 3:16–18 READS: **"For God so loved the world that he gave his one and only Son, that whoever believes in him shall not perish but have eternal life. For God did not send his Son into the world to condemn the world, but to save the world through him. Whoever believes in him is not condemned, but whoever does not believe stands condemned already because he has not believed in the name of God's one and only Son."**

Nicodemus was depending on the Law to get to heaven. By following the Law, he could also give himself the credit for being disciplined and righteous. As he became aware that his way of doing things wouldn't get him into heaven, he was open to hearing God's solution.

Jesus introduced the concept of undeserved grace. For God so loved the world, he gave his one and only Son for the world. Why does God love the world? It's not because we deserved it. God chose to love the world. Because of His love, He designed a foolproof way for fallen humanity to be saved. It would no longer be by human effort. Instead salvation would depend totally on the work of Jesus on the cross.

The plan made no human sense because it was so unfair to Jesus. Why should perfect Jesus, the unblemished lamb, have to pay for the sins of the world? The answer is in the verb "love." John 3:16a tells us that **"For God so loved the world"** that He released Jesus to suffer the penalty of a criminal on death row.

Jesus didn't say "Whoever does this or that" will not be condemned. God was through with our "doing" and missing His holy standards. So, out of grace, He designed a way to replace "whoever does" with "whoever believes." Then, from our relationship of trusting God, we will do the right things.

John 3:34–36 reads: **"For the one whom God has sent speaks the words of God, for God gives the Spirit without limit. The Father loves the Son and has placed everything in his hands. Whoever believes in the Son has eternal life, but whoever rejects the Son will not see life, for God's wrath remains on him."**

John the Baptist tells us in John 3:35b that God the Father **"has placed everything in his hands,"** meaning Jesus gets the final decision as to who makes it to heaven and who doesn't. Jesus paid for our eternal life by dying for us on the cross. He then offered us His sacrifice as full payment of the penalty for our sins. The way we receive the gift of His sacrifice is to believe. John the Baptist said in John 3:36a, "whoever believes in the Son has eternal life."

God the Father hasn't given us the freedom to choose a different way to eternal life. Instead, He left the answer of what happens to us after death to His Son. John the Baptist said in John 3:36b, "whoever rejects the Son will not see life, for God's wrath remains on him." The word "remains" reminds us that God sees our case as already having gone through trial in the heavenly tribunal. The verdict of the Godhead, as it pertained to our sentence, was eternal death! The only way to reverse that verdict is to accept the gift of Jesus. God didn't waive the penalty. What He did was allow Jesus to pay it for us. However, if we choose to reject the Son, then the verdict of death stays the same. That's why John the Baptist said in John 3:36b, "God's wrath remains on him."

The urgency of the decision to accept Jesus lies in the fact that God's wrath is currently on all fallen humanity. So, it's not a situation of being neutral and then incurring God's wrath if we reject Jesus. The situation is, we are on death row and unless we accept Jesus, we will enter eternal death. No one knows how much time we have on earth. Every day we delay in accepting Jesus is a fatal risk we are taking on our lives. What if you don't wake up tomorrow? Do you want God's wrath to "remain" on you when you can settle this very second the removal of His wrath?

Are you ready to accept the gift of Jesus in order to be sure of life after death instead of eternal condemnation? Do you want to live in the power of God's Spirit from now till eternity?

MY APPLICATION

God is perfect love and perfect justice. In His love, He implemented perfect justice by paying the full penalty of our sins. What God wants from me is to receive His gift of salvation and to make choices out of my relationship with Him.

When my son was a preschooler, I stayed up with him all night when he had an asthma attack. I didn't resent being up. I wanted to be up so I could respond quickly if he had trouble breathing. I refused to delegate his care because I felt that no hired help would be as attentive as I was. In the way I serve God, do I stay up to take care of God's business, not because I have to but because I want to? Do I serve out of relationship and not obligation?

When God tells us His wrath remains on those who have not accepted Jesus, He's telling us that He cannot violate His own character of holiness. Sometimes it helps me understand what God has done for me by writing down my prayers. So, here is a prayer to thank God for saving me: "God, thank you for sending Jesus. I understand the verdict on my life was death. I could not wait to get rid of the death sentence that was on me. When I accepted the gift of your son as full payment for my death sentence it was the greatest gift on planet earth! I want to live in the euphoria of that gift for the rest of my life!"

Your application

If you haven't received the gift of God's Son for the full payment of your sins, write how you intend to cover your own mistakes. Explain why you are resistant to God's solution to salvation and insistent on offering your own. If you have accepted God's Son for the full payment of your sins, write your prayer of thanksgiving to God for giving you a chance to move out of His wrath and into His favor. Read your prayer out loud.

WEEKEND
Reflection

MY APPLICATION

Who can I trust enough to share my vulnerabilities? In the past, I could always tell my spiritual father and mother what was going on without fearing they would withdraw their support or use information against me. When someone hurt my feelings, my spiritual father would say, "Don't trust them anymore. If someone betrays you, stop being their friend." His advice was always so concise and so practical. My spiritual mother would say, "Should I go beat them up for you?" The very idea made me laugh because she was petite and fragile. If you walked next to her, you would think the wind could blow her over. How could she beat anyone up?

Because we so enjoyed our journey together, God gave me a saying that I then shared with all supporters of the ministry: "The best part of the journey is YOU!" Indeed, I so enjoyed the relationship with my mentors that I celebrated in every valley and
mountaintop. The relationship made everything better. The victories were shared, and the sorrows felt less painful. Whenever I was depressed, I would call my spiritual father and mother and emotionally bleed all over them. They had

a way of helping me return to the right perspective. Life isn't that bad, they would say, things will be all right. And, indeed, things always did turn out all right. Then they would say, "I wouldn't tell too many people what you just told me!" They were confidantes who protected me. They never wanted anyone to take advantage of my vulnerabilities.

Although my two confidantes were incredible, God was showing me that they didn't have the ability to walk with me into the next level of ministry. God's challenge to me was to let go of an outdated plan in order to reach my destination. They were perfect for the ministry for a season, but God was changing the season. In the same way Nicodemus could no longer rely on the law but had to lean on Jesus, my trust must be in Jesus. He will lead me to my ultimate destination.

Your application

Describe a current situation where things are no longer working like they used to. Say how you must let go of a plan, dated ideas, or a friendship that is past its season. Share how you grieved letting go. Share what you must do to bring closure to the past so you can move on with God's new plan for your life.

5

Discover emotional fulfillment

"It's true that we don't know what we've got until we lose it, but it's also true that we don't know what we've been missing until it arrives."

—*Anonymous*

THE NATIONAL STATISTICS INFORM us that one out of two marriages fail. The disintegration of a marriage carries with it the disintegration of any dreams that went with it. What happened to raising kids together? What happened to building your dream house and using it as a place to bless others? What happened to the promise to be each other's best friend and to be what the other needs you to be for the rest of your lives? No matter what the reason, divorce is painful because anytime a dream dies, you can expect pain to be present.

As a teenager, I daydreamed of the day I would meet my soul mate. In my fantasy, I saw someone whose heart beat as one with mine. He would understand my dreams more than any living being on earth. He would feel all my emotional pain and bind up all my wounds. We would celebrate life together and carry each other through any valley. We would hold on to each other forever and never let go. Then life and reality hit.

Where in the world did I get the criteria for my fantasy soul mate? Was it from Hollywood? Or was it from that deep longing within me to find someone to fill in all the gaps of my emotional needs? It never dawned on me that perhaps the only one who could understand all my needs would be an eternal being who was there through all my past experiences and heartbreaks.

In my twenties, a pastor assured me life would be different if I leaned on Jesus. He said that when God fills the loneliness in my heart, I will operate out of a full emotional reservoir. The idea was, once I have a full emotional reservoir, I'll be able to handle all the challenges of life. It seemed to me that if this was true, then surely the divorce rates among Christians would be lower. Yet, the statistics don't support this statement. In a study by George Barna of the Barna Group, not only did the data indicate little difference in divorce rates between Christians and non-Christians, but the study even indicated the divorce rate was a little higher among Christians. Does this statistic mean Jesus isn't the answer? Or could it be we've lost the fullness of what God wants to give to us?

Having served in women's ministry for over twenty years, I often hear women tell of experiencing utter loneliness in the middle of a marriage. Some call themselves spiritually single because they are married to men who aren't Christians. Others are married to Christian men, but are emotionally disconnected from their husband. So, they are lonely in the middle of a marriage while made to feel guilty by their single friends that they at least have a lifetime companion.

Have you ever been in a place where the person you counted on walked away from you? Have you ever felt the absence of someone so deeply that it dominates your world? It's as if life goes on, but you are parked on the side of the road and can't get going. Could Jesus possibly be the answer to reconcile our past losses and help us reach emotional wholeness?

In John chapter four, in the story of Jesus with the Samaritan woman, Jesus presented Himself as the answer to heal her broken heart from relationships that were no longer part of her life. In her desperate search for love, Jesus offered Himself to her as the Messiah. When she left home to go to the well to draw water, she probably had no idea what miraculous intervention was ahead of her. Are you in a place today where you long for a miraculous intervention? Could it be that today is the day God will touch your life in this lesson?

John 4:4–6 reads: **Now he had to go through Samaria. So he came to a town in Samaria called Sychar, near the plot of ground Jacob had given to his son Joseph. Jacob's well was there, and Jesus, tired as he was**

from the journey, sat down by the well. It was about the sixth hour.

The International Standard Bible Encyclopedia said of the town Sychar, "The manner in which it is mentioned shows that it was not a specially well-known place." In today's words, we might say that it was in the middle of nowhere. Have you ever found yourself in a place that felt disconnected and displaced, so much so that it seemed like you were in the middle of nowhere? Then be encouraged by watching how God worked in Sychar that day!

For it was in Sychar, a place not well-known, that Jesus stopped to rest. Remember, nothing God does is coincidence, and it was in this place that God planned a meeting between Jesus and a woman with a history of broken relationships. Although the town is mentioned once in the Bible and may not have been especially known, John 4:5 tells us it had historical significance because it was **"near the plot of ground Jacob had given to his son Joseph."**

The International Standard Bible Encyclopedia says of Joseph, "Joseph stands out among the patriarchs in some respects with preeminence. His nobility of character, his purity of heart and life, his magnanimity as a ruler and brother Patriarch make him, more than any other of the Old Testament characters, an illustration of that type of man which Christ was to give to the world in perfection."

Did the Samaritan woman know she was near the plot of ground Jacob had given to Joseph, a chosen and revered leader in God's spiritual history?

Did you know that you could be located next to a major church or in a city where God has done great things and yet have missed finding God in your life? We can be so close and yet so far. In the midst of the miraculous that is taking place around us, we could be living in a personal desert. What God wants is a miracle that takes place inside of you. Are you a miracle waiting to happen?

John 4:6 also tells us that Sychar was near where "Jacob's well" was dug. The International Standard Bible Encyclopedia provides additional information on Jacob's well. It says, "We must remember that in the East, very strict laws have always governed the use of water, especially when there were large herds to be considered…The patriarch, therefore, may have dug the well in the interests of peace, and also to preserve his own independence."

If, indeed, Jacob dug his own well in the interest of peace, the setting was perfect for Jesus to show the Samaritan woman how God has the answer to resolve conflict in her life and grant her peace. She probably had no idea about the spiritual significance of where she was standing. What about you? Are you sitting in a Bible study? Are you reading this book filled with God's Word? Do you have any idea how close you are to receiving God's healing from His Word?

John 4:7–9 reads: **When a Samaritan woman came to draw water, Jesus said to her, "Will you give me a drink?" (His disciples had gone into the town to buy food.) The Samaritan woman said to him, "You are a Jew and I am a Samaritan woman. How can you ask me for a drink?" (For Jews do not associate with Samaritans.)**

Jesus' disciples had gone into town to buy food. This left Jesus at the well. The Samaritan woman who came to draw water had her eyes on the well and the water. She intentionally ignored Jesus because she was conditioned to expect that Samaritans and Jews didn't associate with each other. She was surprised when Jesus spoke to her. Not only did He speak to her, but He asked her for a drink of water.

Have you ever been in a place in your life when you didn't expect anyone to speak to you because you had nothing left to give? Never in a million years would you expect to hear from God after the mess you've made. Don't be so quick to write God off as wanting nothing to do with you. While you may have given up on ever being emotionally whole, God isn't through with you. He can fill your heart in a way you never imagined!

Jesus asked the Samaritan woman for a cup of water, while she'd never expected a Jew to ask her for anything. When God speaks to us, He redefines the rules. He defies expectations. Have you ever been surprised by a request from God for your resources?

God is Master over any culture, so He reserves the right to rewrite the cultural rules. He isn't bound by the prejudices of our fallen humanity. He isn't even bound by our self-image. Has God ever inquired about a resource you possessed when you felt you were in a personal wilderness? How incredible to witness that God begins restoration by showing us we have something to give. From what we have to offer, He then pours more into us so we can pour out His hope to others.

John 4:10–12 reads: **Jesus answered her, "If you knew the gift of God and who it is that asks you for a drink, you would have asked him and he would have given you living water." "Sir," the woman said, "you have nothing to draw with and the well is deep. Where can you get**

this living water? Are you greater than our father Jacob, who gave us the well and drank from it himself, as did also his sons and his flocks and herds?"

The woman didn't catch on that Jesus was speaking of spiritual life. She assessed Jesus in the context of physical water. First, He had asked her for water. Now, He was offering her water. How could He give her water since He had nothing to draw water with? She then inquired who Jesus was. Was He greater than Jacob, who dug the well? Her question implied, "And if, indeed, you are greater than our father, Jacob, then who does that make you?"

John 4:13–14 reads: **Jesus answered, "Everyone who drinks this water will be thirsty again, but whoever drinks the water I give him will never thirst. Indeed, the water I give him will become in him a spring of water welling up to eternal life."**

The woman focused on the physical well and water while Jesus was offering her Himself as the fountain of living waters. I wonder if there are times we focus on the external when what we really need is to feel accepted and loved. More than the acceptance of each other, what we need most is God's acceptance.

So, perhaps we find ourselves arguing over getting the perfect house or the perfect car. We might get upset because the gift we received was not exactly what we wanted. Our focus might be on the externals when, deep down, we are expressing an emotional insecurity. We might be measuring someone's love by what they give us, but the real love we are looking for cannot be measured by a physical gift—it's a connection of the heart.

In my relationships with my sons, I have found that my husband is more secure than me. If the boys forget to call, he immediately thinks something isn't right. He has no doubt that they'd call if everything was fine. I, on the other hand, immediately think they've forgotten me. I respond out of my own emotional needs. But, oh, how I long for the security my husband experiences. His emotional reservoir is full, and it shows in how he responds to life.

Jesus wanted to take the Samaritan woman into a deeper place of emotional fulfillment. In John 4:14, what Jesus was offering the Samaritan woman was the inner peace and satisfaction of God's acceptance that can be compared to a "spring of water welling up to eternal life." Have you been seeking guarantees in the physical realm when true freedom and peace comes from God's guarantee of your eternal acceptance into His kingdom? What need have you repeatedly failed to satisfy? Perhaps your repeated failure is a clue that you are trying to fulfill the wrong need. Or perhaps you are looking to the wrong person to meet your need.

John 4:15–18 reads: **The woman said to him, "Sir, give me this water so that I won't get thirsty and have to keep coming here to draw water." He told her, "Go, call your husband and come back." "I have no husband," she replied. Jesus said to her, "You are right when you say you have no husband. The fact is, you have had five husbands, and the man you now have is not your husband. What you have just said is quite true."**

In the Old Testament, the well was a meeting place where some key women found husbands. How interesting that, for a woman who had five husbands and was currently in an unmarried relationship, that God should set her meeting place with Jesus at a well. Jesus knew that deep in her heart hid a longing for a husband who would be true to her. God was giving her the perfect husband in Jesus!

In the Old Testament, Genesis 24:12–15 tells us that Isaac's wife, Rebecca, was discovered by Abraham's servant at a well. Genesis 29:1–11 tells us that Jacob met Rachel at a well. Exodus 2:16–21 tells us Moses met his wife at a well. And now, in John 4, we have the Samaritan woman at the well, a woman whose personal life evidenced her failure to find a good husband. As she meets Jesus there, she discovers a husband who is also her Maker.

What about you? Do you long for a perfect soul mate? What relationship are you looking for? God wants to be the relationship that fills our deepest longings.

Isaiah 54:5 reads: **For your Maker is your husband—the LORD Almighty is his name—the Holy One of Israel is your Redeemer; he is called the God of all the earth.**

MY APPLICATION

God, my Maker, is my husband. When I got married to my Prince Charming, I was in a state of panic when I discovered he couldn't take away my emotional pain. He was in a panic because he was lost as to how to make my pain go away. Finally, we both turned to God because we knew that whatever was wrong, only He could fix. Years later, my husband still tells the story. He said he thought all I needed was someone to love me, and that his love would bring my healing. He was sure I would be fine in six months. Today, he's first to say that there are deep emotional scars from my background that will not have quick fixes. It will require a lifetime of nursing and extraordinary love. Today, he no longer asks, "Why did that incident trigger your pain?" Instead, he simply trusts God will see me through it.

At the same time, I have discovered that, as perfect as my husband is (and I don't exaggerate when I say he is perfect for me and for my family), I still sometimes wake up to a deep sense of loneliness. I don't know if it was left by the way my mother abruptly exited from my life. I just know the pain still surfaces after all these years. The good news is, when I feel the pain, I immediately turn to Jesus as the one who will fill all the lonely places in my heart. He not only gives me eternal life, but He gives me abundant life while on earth. So, when I am in emotional pain, I open the Bible. I meditate on God's Word. I listen for the voice of Jesus. I let God remind me that Jesus loved me so much He chose to die for me. I bask in the perfection of His love until the pain goes away.

Your application

Describe a time someone hurt your feelings or when a relationship you counted on could not meet your need the way you had hoped. Share how God met the need in ways no person could.

DAY 1

GIVE GOD A CHANCE TO SHOW

YOU HIS MERCY AND KINDNESS—

DON'T LET BAD ENCOUNTERS

WITH RELIGIOUS PEOPLE KEEP

YOU FROM GOD.

———◆———

JOHN 4:19–20 READS: **"Sir," the woman said, "I can see that you are a prophet. Our fathers worshiped on this mountain, but you Jews claim that the place where we must worship is in Jerusalem."**

The woman called Jesus a prophet because He knew personal details about her life. She didn't understand why this prophet wanted anything to do with her. Her insecurity was a result of the history between the Samaritans and the Jews. Have you ever allowed negative past experiences with the church to keep you from a relationship with God?

In John 4:20, the Samaritan woman refers to this negative cultural history.

Let's take a quick review of the history of Samaria. When the people of Israel were exiled in Assyria, 2 Kings 17:24–26 tells us that the king of Assyria **"brought people from Babylon, Cuthah, Avva, Hamath, and Sepharvaim and settled them in the towns of Samaria to replace the Israelites. When they first lived there, they did not worship the LORD."**

We are told that it was reported to the king of Assyria, **"The people you deported and resettled in the towns of Samaria do not know what the god of that country requires. He has sent lions among them, which are killing them off, because the people do not know what he requires."**

In order to win God's favor, the king of Assyria decided to send back to Samaria one of the Jewish priests who had been exiled. 2 Kings 17:27 tells us, **Then the king of Assyria gave this order: "Have one of the priests you took captive from Samaria go back to live there and teach the people what the god of the land requires."** The reason for sending a priest back to the people was to teach them how to worship God in order to secure His protection. However, the hearts of the people were not pure. They mixed worshipping God with worshipping their own gods. The only reason they worshipped the God of the Israelites was to keep from being attacked by lions. 2 Kings 17:33 tells us, **"They worshiped the LORD, but they also served their own gods in accordance with the customs of the nations from which they had been brought."**

When those who had been exiled returned to Jerusalem and were rebuilding the temple, Ezra 4:1–3 tells us that the resettled Samaritans offered to help. Ezra 4:3 tells us that **Zerubbabel, Jeshua, and the rest of the heads of the families of Israel answered, "You have no part with us in building a temple to our God. We alone will build it for the LORD, the God of Israel, as King Cyrus, the king of Persia, commanded us."**

The enmity between the Samaritans and the Jews increased as a result of their exclusion from rebuilding the temple. The Jews didn't see them as fit to be part of the project because of how they mingled their worship with other gods.

The Samaritan woman was telling Jesus that the Samaritans were excluded from the rebuilding of the temple in Jerusalem. They, therefore, worshipped on their own mountain while the Jews worshipped in their temple. Why was He talking to her, since the Samaritans were never seen as worthy of having a part of God?

MY APPLICATION

As I reflect on my experiences with Christians, there were some great Christians I met along the way whose actions could have totally destroyed my faith. I've experienced times when someone excluded me because I was a woman. I've had people reject me because I wasn't from their hometown. But, thank God, His Spirit continued to draw me. Somehow, God impressed in my heart that I needed to make my assessment of Him based on the truths revealed in the Bible. Fellow Christians have seldom been a good billboard to advertise who God is.

When I finished seminary, I had buried my head in studies for years. I had lived in a totally artificial world in the library, as compared to the real world. Or perhaps I should say that, in the Bible, I saw a glimpse of the world God intended. Then, when I emerged into life around me, there was very little resemblance to the world God wanted. At first, I was disillusioned and wanted to give up. Then God showed me I wasn't alone. He was raising up servants to represent His heart to the world. Just because I had bad experiences with some Christians didn't mean God had let me down. I needed to stop letting imperfect people define my world. I, too, would mess up. So, I pray that I will never be a stumbling block to someone who is watching my life. At the end of the day, we all need a Savior, not only for our salvation but for our sanctification. It is only through Jesus that any of us stands a chance of living a life that honors God.

YOUR APPLICATION

Describe a time a Christian's wrong choices or a church's decision caused you to be disillusioned with God and ministry. Share how knowing that Jesus offered the Samaritan woman a positive spiritual encounter encourages you in your life.

DAY 2

Devotion

GOING THROUGH THE MOTIONS

LEAVES US FEELING EMPTY-

HEARTED—WORSHIP GOD IN

A WAY THAT FILLS YOUR HEART

WITH RELATIONSHIP.

———————

JOHN 4:21–24 READS: **Jesus declared, "Believe me, woman, a time is coming when you will worship the Father neither on this mountain nor in Jerusalem. You Samaritans worship what you do not know; we worship what we do know, for salvation is from the Jews. Yet a time is coming and has now come when the true worshipers will worship the Father in spirit and truth, for they are the kind of worshipers the Father seeks. God is spirit, and his worshipers must worship in spirit and in truth."**

The Samaritan woman told Jesus that the Samaritans were excluded from the rebuilding of the temple in Jerusalem. They worshipped on their own mountain while the Jews worshipped in their temple. Why, then, was He talking to her, since the Samaritans were never seen as worthy of having a part of God?

In John 4:22b, Jesus stated that salvation "is from the Jews." God does not apologize for choosing the Jews as His chosen people from whom the Messiah would come. Jesus said in John 4:22a the "Samaritans worship what you do not know" because it was through the Jews that they were introduced to the true God. However, what Jesus wanted was to get past the background and to focus on the choice we will make today. The history that led to our knowledge of God is not as important as what we will do in our relationship with God today.

Jesus was telling the Samaritan woman that He was fully aware of the history. His assessment was that the Samaritans needed to offer God true worship. The International Standard Bible Encyclopedia said, "When it suited their purpose the Samaritans claimed relationship with the Jews, asserting that their roll of the Pentateuch was the only authentic copy; they were equally ready to deny all connection in times of stress, and even to dedicate their temple to a heathen deity."

God is through with our dabbling in worship. He wants true worship that evidences our relationship with Him. Have you ever worshipped God only because you needed something from Him? God isn't pleased with this kind of worship. He is offended when we use Him for our purpose, without really caring about Him. God wants us to worship Him because He is worthy of our love and adoration.

Jesus was telling the Samaritan woman that she needed to let go of the old way of doing things. True worship will not be found in the temple of the Samaritans, nor will it be found in the temple the Jews built. True worship will be found in the hearts of those who sincerely seek God and believe Him to be worthy of their praise. In John 4:24b Jesus states that what God wants are those who worship **"in spirit and in truth."**

The worship God wants from us is not some kind of insurance plan we throw into the mix just in case God is the answer. True worship is not a heart that thinks, "Why not add a prayer in case it helps?" God is not some good luck charm. He wants a heart that is truthful, with a spirit that says, "I will go to God because He is the only one who has the right answers for my life. I will thank God because He is the only one who offers me true relationship that feeds my soul."

My application

God wants true worship, not a worship that cries out to Him only when He can meet my needs. I confess that, for many years of my Christian life, I looked to God because of what He could do for me. Over time, God impressed on my heart the meaning of true worship. It is the act of praising and honoring God for who He is. His holiness is worthy of honor. His justice is worthy of honor. His mercy is worthy of honor. His actions that result from His holiness, justice, and mercy are worthy of honor. God doesn't have to do one more thing for me and He remains worthy of honor. Worship is all about God, not all about me.

I also learned that we can worship God, not only with the praise from our mouths, but with the way we live. When we choose to be a holy vessel, that can be our worship. When we choose to sacrifice, that can be our worship. Worship is whatever we do to shout to the world that God is worthy of both our successes as well as our sufferings. In fact, I have learned that God is the one who designs our worship. For Jesus, God the Father chose the cross. Jesus worshipped God perfectly by staying on the cross till His mission was over. What's the ultimate worship I can offer God? I know extravagant worship will cost me. At the end of my life, I desire to lay at God's feet a worship that is fitting for a king. So, God gets to decide the worship He wants. No matter what God designs, my prayer is that I will be willing. Oh, I pray God will receive the worship He desires, and that I will not be a reluctant worshipper!

YOUR APPLICATION

Share how true worship will be expressed in your life. What can you do to show your utmost adoration of God? Say how worshipping God can include giving up your greatest need and trusting God to meet it similarly to the Samaritan woman, who laid down her deepest emotional need and found her relationship in Jesus.

Day 3

Devotion

ANALYSIS PARALYSIS CAN KEEP

US IN A PARCHED LAND—WHEN

GOD HAS SPOKEN, WHAT ELSE

ARE WE WAITING FOR?

———————

John 4:25–27 reads: **The woman said, "I know that Messiah" (called Christ) "is coming. When he comes, he will explain everything to us." Then Jesus declared, "I who speak to you am he." Just then his disciples returned and were surprised to find him talking with a woman. But no one asked, "What do you want?" or "Why are you talking with her?"**

The woman lived for so long with one husband after another that, chances are, most of her life hadn't been one she displayed openly. Jesus was asking for a worship that was truthful. If you've lived a lie most of your life, the idea of revealing your heart to God **"in spirit and in truth"** as described in John 4:24 might create panic. The woman clearly wasn't ready for such transparency. So, she put Jesus off by saying in John 4:25, **"I know that Messiah (called Christ) is coming. When he comes he will explain everything to us."**

Jesus didn't allow the woman to procrastinate anymore. He could have said, "Enough revelation for one day; let's just give her time to absorb everything." There are times when God gives us information and lets us ponder what He has revealed. Then there are times when God has given us the key information we need in order to make a decision. Jesus cuts through all the details with His summation statement in John 4:26, **"I who speak to you am he."** After this declaration, the ball was in the woman's court.

Is God asking you for a decision? We can either say "Yes" to God and receive His blessing, or we can say "No" and trust in our old ways. There are times God may ask for a decision and, if we say no, there will not be a second chance.

John 4:27a tells us that **"Just then his disciples returned."** Why did the disciples return "just then?" Just when did they return? There was nothing else Jesus had to say to the Samaritan woman. It was the perfect time for the disciples to return because the conversation was over. All that was left was her decision. Will she believe Jesus is the Messiah and receive His living waters?

My application

When God has said all He has to say, the next move is ours. When God showed me that life wasn't about finding my soul mate in this world, but in letting Him be my soul mate, I had to let go of the ideas I had for a perfect earthly relationship. I had to transition into seeing people as individuals God sends into my life for a season. However, the lasting relationship is with God Himself. Any time I give someone a place in my life at the expense of throwing God out, I set myself up for a setback. The only way to live on a solid foundation is to put my hands in the hands of an eternal husband. I struggle with this because I'm such a people person. So, when I find myself getting too attached to anyone, I intentionally withdraw and spend more isolated time with God. Then, when I emerge from my spiritual retreat, I am stronger. I also relate better to others when I operate out of a full emotional reservoir, compared to being desperate for someone to affirm me.

When my sons were growing up, I found myself growing too emotionally attached to them. I didn't want to suffocate them with my emotional needs. So, I intentionally created physical distance by filling up my time with other activities. All the while, I was watching from afar to make sure they were doing fine. I made sure my husband was at all their activities because as long as there was one parent present, I was at peace. Unlike me, my husband had the ability to spend time with my sons without becoming emotionally dependent on them. For example, he could objectively counsel them to go to the best college, even if it meant going out-of-state. I, on the other hand, would have clung to them and wanted them to go to a college within driving distance of home. Over time, as I developed my relationship with Christ, I found myself more able to get closer to those I love without overwhelming them with my emotional needs.

YOUR APPLICATION

Describe a time when you became dependent on someone to the point that you couldn't function without him or her. Share how you can redirect your time and focus to build a solid foundation in God Himself.

DAY 4

SOME DECISIONS REQUIRE MORE

INFORMATION, OTHERS REQUIRE

MORE TRUST—YOU DON'T NEED

TO KNOW ALL THE FACTS BEFORE

TRUSTING GOD.

———

JESUS STOPPED TO SPEAK TO A WOMAN IN SAMARIA. GOD'S blessing of Jesus was not restricted to the Jews. In the Old Testament, God had reiterated His promise to Jacob in Genesis 28:14 that "**Your descendants will be like the dust of the earth, and you will spread out to the west and to the east, to the north and to the south. All peoples on earth will be blessed through you and your offspring.**" Jesus reached out to a Samaritan woman as evidence of God's promise that the Messiah would save the world. How did she respond? How did you respond to God's offer?

John 4:28–30 reads: **Then, leaving her water jar, the woman went back to the town and said to the people, "Come, see a man who told me everything I ever did. Could this be the Christ?" They came out of the town and made their way toward him.**

Some people process by going away and quietly meditating on what took place. Others process by telling people what happened, even when they are unsure as to what just happened. Observe that she didn't tell everyone that she'd met the Christ. Instead, she referred to Jesus in John 4:29 as "a man who told me everything I ever did."

Observe that the woman said in John 4:29b, **"Could this be the Christ?"** Did you know that you don't need to be sure of all the details before sharing your experience with others? The woman focused on what she knew and reinforced what she knew by sharing this detail with others. When we build on the truth we know, God will take us into deeper faith. But we must begin somewhere.

John 4:39–42 reads: **Many of the Samaritans from that town believed in him because of the woman's testimony, "He told me everything I ever did." So when the Samaritans came to him, they urged him to stay with them, and he stayed two days. And because of his words many more became believers. They said to the woman, "We no longer believe just because of what you said; now we have heard for ourselves, and we know that this man really is the Savior of the world."**

The Samaritan woman didn't testify to Jesus being the Messiah. Yet because of her testimony about her encounter with Jesus, John 4:39–40 tells us that **"Many of the**

Samaritans from that town believed in him because of the woman's testimony, 'He told me everything I ever did.'"

All the Samaritan woman did was share what she was sure of. God can use our testimony to draw others to Him even when we are unsure of all the details. Once the people were drawn to Jesus, they had their own personal encounter with Him. John 4:40b tells us **"they urged him to stay with them, and he stayed two days."** God is perfectly able to defend His own reputation. After the people spent two days with Jesus, John 4:41b tells us **"many more became believers."** Is there someone you need to invite to a spiritual event or activity where they can have their own encounter with Jesus?

The fact that "many more became believers" also tells us that she too became a believer as well. The idea being many more followed in her footsteps and became believers. The Samarian woman began with saying Jesus was a man who knew details about her. She went from this revelation to believing with the others who stated in John 4:42b that Jesus was **"the Savior of the world."**

My application

The Samaritan woman started sharing her personal encounter with God. I believe this is the sincerest place to start. I used to think I had to answer every question about God before I could tell others about Him. Perhaps I was afraid to be challenged and to feel silly if I didn't have an answer to every possible question. But God wanted me to know that I cannot share what I don't know. I can only begin with what has happened to me.

When I was a young believer, I didn't know God's Word that well. However, I could tell the world that, as an immigrant, I experienced leaving my country and walking into a different world. During that time, I could almost feel the arms of God around me. He was there when I cried out to Him. When I was a sophomore in college, I had transferred to a new college. I didn't know anyone and cried out to God to put me in the right community. During the break in between class, a girl walked up to me, introduced herself, and welcomed me into her network. When I transferred to graduate school, I was once again in a new city and didn't know a soul. This time, I became impatient and ran ahead of God to take care of my own social needs. I don't know why. It must've been human pride, thinking I could solve my own problems. Maybe I felt I had exhausted my quota of miracles. I ended up in a complicated relationship and hurt myself, as well as those around me. If someone were to ask me in my college years how to find the will of God, I would not have been able to help them like I could today. All I could share then was my personal experience with God. God has shown me that we can begin by our personal encounters with God and leave the rest up to Him.

YOUR APPLICATION

Describe a personal encounter you had with God where He met a need in your life. What were you struggling with and what answer did God give you that changed your perspective and choices? Did you keep God's deliverance to yourself? Describe how you shared your good news with others.

DAY 5
Devotion

LIFE CAN BE FILLED WITH

ROUTINE ACTIVITIES—IN THE

MIDST OF YOUR PRACTICAL

SCHEDULE, DON'T MISS STEPPING

INTO THE MIRACULOUS.

——————

JOHN 4:31–34 READS: **Meanwhile his disciples urged him, "Rabbi, eat something." But he said to them, "I have food to eat that you know nothing about." Then his disciples said to each other, "Could someone have brought him food?" "My food," said Jesus, "is to do the will of him who sent me and to finish his work."**

The Samaritan woman thought Jesus was speaking of physical water when He referred to spiritual waters. This isn't just the case with her, but is the case with many believers. Similar to the Samaritan woman, Jesus' disciples thought He was referring to physical bread when He was referring to spiritual sustenance by obeying God's will.

Both the Samaritan woman and Jesus' disciples missed the significance of His words. Jesus gave them fact after fact that aligned with what God said about the Messiah. They were right next to Jesus and missed who He was.

Isaiah 55:1–2 reads: **"Come, all you who are thirsty, come to the waters; and you who have no money, come, buy and eat! Come, buy wine and milk without money and without cost. Why spend money on what is not bread, and your labor on what does not satisfy? Listen, listen to me, and eat what is good, and your soul will delight in the richest of fare."**

What about you? Are you standing next to one of God's servants while totally missing the power of God that is being offered to you?

John 4:35–38 reads: **"Do you not say, 'Four months more and then the harvest?' I tell you, open your eyes and look at the fields! They are ripe for harvest. Even now the reaper draws his wages, even now he harvests the crop for eternal life, so that the sower and the reaper may be glad together. Thus the saying 'One sows and another reaps' is true. I sent you to reap what you have not worked for. Others have done the hard work, and you have reaped the benefits of their labor."**

The Samaritan woman tried to put off believing in Christ by referring to a future time when the Messiah would come. The disciples already believed, but the sin of believers is not one of unbelief, but of procrastination. God didn't want the Samaritan woman to put off the decision to believe in

Jesus, nor does He want believers to put off obedience in doing His will.

When Jesus said in John 4:35b to "open your eyes and look at the fields," He was telling the disciples to pay attention to the miraculous activity of God that was already on the schedule. The field that is ready for harvest showcases what has been happening under the soil. It is the revelation of a miracle that has been working all along. Perhaps you think nothing is happening, but God is telling us that something is already happening. What God wants us to do is to reap the harvest.

Has the miracle been taking place inside you? Has the miracle been taking place inside those around you? Don't underestimate God. Instead believe Him. God is inviting you to look at the fields. This time, look at the fields with His eyes. God does not see bare fields. He sees the fruit. He sees the harvest. What about you?

MY APPLICATION

God tells us the fields are ready for the harvest. This tells me God's Spirit has been working. So, when I look out at the fields and life seems bleak, this is a lie of the Devil. God wants me to look with eyes of faith. God is all about bearing fruit. He can transform any soil. He can make any seed grow. If I am concerned over my children, I need to trust

God to bear fruit from the seeds of faith that have been sown into them. If I am concerned about a ministry, I need to trust that God wants ministries to flourish. God is sure of His desire to reach the world. His Spirit will stir the hearts of those who share God's love for the world. He wants to draw as many as possible into His kingdom. I don't have to force anything to happen. I just need to fan into flame what is already happening.

I recall a time when the ministry needed help. With my physical eyes, I couldn't see anyone willing to help. Then God surprised me by raising up a newcomer who responded to the need. I couldn't understand why someone new to the ministry was the one who took care of the need. God showed me that there was already activity in that believer's life because the Holy Spirit had been at work. In other words, though I couldn't see the activity under the surface, seeds of faith had already been planted. God timed the harvest in that believer's life at the exact time when our ministry needed the fruit.

YOUR APPLICATION

Describe a bleak situation you experienced and share how
the projection of a harvest gives you renewed hope and motivation to serve all the more. Share what you can do to
prepare the ground, to sow the seed, or to keep the crops
watered so the harvest can be full.

WEEKEND
Reflection

MY APPLICATION

When God appoints you to a mission, did you know you can lead, even with a bleeding heart? In the midst of my grieving the loss of my spiritual father and the declining health of my spiritual mother, God continued to work in me and through me. The ministry celebrated its successes. Meanwhile, I could no longer call my spiritual father because God had brought him home. I greatly missed calling my spiritual mother, knowing she could no longer talk on the phone.

A friend of mine advised me to allow myself to grieve. My preference would have been to stuff the pain. I found it took more courage to feel the pain. After every visit with my spiritual mother, I allowed my mind to recycle over her daily involvement in my life for the past twelve years.

There was hardly a day that went by when she didn't require me to give her a full report of my day and provided spiritual insight on how I responded to life's challenges. When I responded according to God's Word, she would say, "Good girl!" and started clapping. When she disapproved of my attitude or lack of faith, she would say, "Should we ask God for more faith?" She made me a plaque that read "Anita, trust me in this, I have everything under control. Your loving heavenly Daddy." To the public, I came across with boldness. With her, I felt like the person in the song, "This warrior is but a child."

God had to remind me that while He allowed me to have a spiritual father and mother, He ultimately was the one who walked with me. They served as encouragers, but they weren't physically present as I confronted the challenges to the ministry. They served as cheerleaders and prayer warriors, but I still had to enter the battlefield. It was God who gave me the words and the wisdom to build Inspire Women from zero in the bank to being a perpetual ministry. God reminded me that my spiritual mother used to say, "I'll pray and you jump out of the plane without a parachute!" She would say, "Don't you dare stop!" However, the reality was, she wasn't there in person to face the giants. I used to tease her by saying, "It's much easier to fight battles in a prayer closet. How about I pray this time, and you jump?"

Only God could have carried me through the challenges. Ultimately, He is my best friend and has been the one all along who empowered me. More than that, I had to learn what the Samaritan woman did when she found Jesus. She didn't dwell on the relationships in her past. She also didn't just sit with her new-found relationship. Instead, she went into the community to tell people about Jesus. Her activity was what bore fruit. In the same way, God showed me that the worst thing I can do is to stop sharing His message. My strength will come from staying focused on the mission. When life is uncertain, the one thing I can control is my certainty to keep going in God's mission. The worst thing I can do is to just sit and dwell on the earthly relationships I've lost. It is in my sharing my relationship with God and seeing other people transformed that my heart will be full again. To keep my heart full, I must not let God become an event in the past but an active vibrant force in the present.

YOUR APPLICATION

Describe a current emotional need you have. Perhaps you're looking for a soul mate. Perhaps you're looking for the approval of a boss or affirmation from a loved one. Perhaps you long to be invited into a neighborhood, community, or church circle. Share how you may have denied having an emotional need because it has gone unmet for some time. Share how knowing that Jesus sees the need and wants to meet it has made a difference.

6

Settle those lingering questions

"When you feel like giving up, remember why
you held on for so long in the first place."

~ Anonymous

W HEN I WAS ABOUT eleven years old, I remember sitting by the window, waiting for a new puppy to arrive. I was told that a friend decided to find a new home for the puppy, and that my parents had offered to take it. My parents weren't sure when the puppy would be delivered, but said it would be some time on Saturday. So, I sat by the window all Saturday and waited with anticipation. I refused to have lunch. I wasn't going to miss this great moment. I wanted to absorb every second of it.

By four in the afternoon, I began to show weariness. It's not easy to sit on a window sill for that long. By six in the afternoon, doubt started to creep in. By the time the sun went down, I was filled with disappointment and confusion. What happened? Did the people change their minds about finding a new home for the puppy? Did someone else offer to take it? Scenarios cycled through my head. Finally, my father broke the news and said, "Your mother told them we didn't want the puppy!" I was stunned. Why did she let me sit on the window sill all day? Incidents like that make me afraid to ever even dare to wish. As I look back now, I can see that from an early age, I was conditioned to think that wishes didn't come true!

Thank God I don't think that way anymore! Since then, God has entered my life and totally remapped my world. Over the years, I've discovered that He is a God who believes in dreams coming true. He is a God who has the courage to repair His own dreams. Nothing is too big a mess for God to restore! As we are made in His image, we have within us the courage to finish a dream as well.

Where are you in your life today? What does your heart long for? Perhaps you feel crippled in your family because no one listens to you. Perhaps you feel crippled in your work because you don't have the right resources to reach your goals. Have you been waiting for so long that you've lost all expectations? Then perhaps today is a great day for God to show up. Jesus was God's answer to repair His dream. Could Jesus be yours? Let's find out together.

John 5:1–6 reads: **Some time later, Jesus went up to Jerusalem for a feast of the Jews. Now there is in Jerusalem** near the Sheep Gate a pool, which in Aramaic is called Bethesda and which is surrounded by five covered colonnades. Here a great number of disabled people used to lie—the blind, the lame, the paralyzed. One who was there had been an invalid for thirty-eight years. When Jesus saw him lying there and learned that he had been in this condition for a long time, he asked him, "Do you want to get well?"

During the time when a religious feast was going on, John 5:1b tells us Jesus went to a **"feast of the Jews."** Nelson's Illustrated Bible Dictionary tells us that "The feasts and festivals of the Jewish nation were scheduled at specific times in the annual calendar." We are also told that "Some marked the beginning or the end of the agricultural year, while others commemorated historic events in the life of the nation. All of the feasts were marked by thanksgiving and joyous feasting."

It isn't clear as to what this feast was. However, given the nature of feasts, we know that this feast occurred annually at a specific time.

When an event occurs on a regular basis, attendees might have the attitude of "same time last year, same time this year, same time next year." Have you ever gone through the motions of a religious season—such as Easter or Christmas—without expecting God to move in a miraculous way? Have you ever dragged yourself out of bed and gone to church, not expecting much from God?

It was during the time of an annual religious feast designed for joy and thanksgiving that we find Jesus going to Jerusalem. John 5:3b tells us He finds a **"great number of** disabled people" by a pool of water. The crowd was by the pool as usual. "Bethesda" means House of Mercy. However, there was no sense that anyone expected mercy. Have you ever been in a place that was once known for God's miraculous intervention, only to sit with a lack of expectation?

The disabled people in this story were found within the perimeters of five covered colonnades. In John 5:3 we are told the category of "disabled" people included "the blind, the lame, the paralyzed." Because of his handicap, the lame man fit the disabled category…at least, on the outside. But, unlike the rest, he was wearing a hidden label that marked him as God's miracle-about-to-happen.

Perhaps you've been labeled as divorced, widowed, unemployed, or in transition. Perhaps you've been grouped in the category of those filing for bankruptcy. Perhaps you've been labeled as having bipolar disease, high blood pressure, diabetes, or cancer. Like the lame man in this story, it might appear like you belong to the category of the disabled or the challenged. No matter what category the world has put you in, God can hide a label in you that reads, "Marked for a miracle."

When, in the Book of Ruth, Naomi was going back to her country after her husband and sons died, she labeled herself as "bitter." Can you hear her saying over and over again, "Why me?" But God had already marked her as a woman of His favor. Naomi began her time of loss and transition in Ruth 1:20–21: **"Don't call me Naomi," she told them. "Call me Mara, because the Almighty has made my life very bitter. I went away full, but the LORD has brought me back empty. Why call me Naomi? The**

LORD has afflicted me; the Almighty has brought misfortune upon me." By the time God was through working in Naomi's life, the story ended as recorded in Ruth 4:16–17: **Then Naomi took the child, laid him in her lap and cared for him. The women living there said, "Naomi has a son." And they named him Obed. He was the father of Jesse, the father of David.** Naomi's question, "Why call me Naomi?" ended in a God transformed celebration.

Jesus came from the line of David. Can you imagine the woman who called herself "bitter" being chosen for the line from which the Messiah came? What about you? I wonder if today is the day God will show you the grandeur of your future.

In the book of John, chapter 5, we know that Jesus asked about the lame man because God's Word tells us in John 5:6 that Jesus "**learned that he had been in this condition for a long time.**" To inquire about the man, Jesus had to first zero in on him. Just imagine God walking in the crowd and picking one person to inquire about. If God were to pick one person, do you want that person to be you?

Now, imagine God inquiring about you. What would people say about you? How would they describe your needs? Perhaps you've been putting on such a strong front that no one has any idea what's going on inside you. The great news is, Jesus is now seated at the right hand of God the Father in heaven. I would love to eavesdrop on His conversation with the Father and the Holy Spirit. Imagine Him saying, "Look over there. See what's going on. Let's intervene in her life." When God inquires about you, He does something with the answer. He doesn't gossip. He takes the information and makes an executive decision that will change your life.

When God looks at you during a time of need, you are in a place of favor. There are times we cannot explain why God stopped to address our needs when there are so many other needs around us. In John 5, there were many disabled people under the colonnade. Yet, God zeroed in on one to inquire and to show favor. Could today be the day God looks at you?

When one of my sons was looking for a job, I prayed for him, and we all celebrated when he got the job. He said to me, "Does God answer the prayers of everyone who asks for a job?" I knew he was trying to decide if he got the job based on God's intervention, or if the prayers sent for him were merely coincidence. I said, "Son, you don't have to worry about what God does with everyone else. Don't analyze God right out of your life. All you need to know is that God touched your life. So praise Him for it!"

Are you looking at all the other disabled people around you and talking yourself right out of a miracle? Instead of focusing on statistics and probabilities, it's time to stop discouraging yourself by looking at all the needs out there. Just be honest with God about your need.

During my senior year in high school, I was disconnected from my real needs. If you asked those around me, they would probably assess me as being successful. My teachers voted me as the student most likely to succeed. They didn't know that, at the time, I was dying emotionally. I missed my mother terribly, but was afraid to tell anyone. I was trying to pretend that I was doing fine.

Once you admit your need, the next question is, what do you want to do about it? God will not force healing on us. Before intervening in the invalid's life, Jesus asked him in John 5:6b, **"Do you want to get well?"** This may be a surprise to you, but not everyone wants to get well. There are times when we are so used to not having our needs met that our state of desperation becomes part of our identity.

Have you ever seen a canary when the birdcage door is open? Instead of flying away, the bird stays in the cage or walks around the outside of it. The fact is, our limitations can become so comfortable that the idea of not having them actually scares us!

When I lost my mother, I was stuck in limbo in the middle of a tragic loss. I didn't realize that, subconsciously, I felt guilty to move on. I felt I was dishonoring my mother if I moved on too quickly. I thought my grief was my best way to honor her. The truth was, she wouldn't have wanted me to waste my life in depression. My best way to honor her was to live a full life.

In response to Jesus' question, John 5:7 reads: **"Sir," the invalid replied, "I have no one to help me into the pool when the water is stirred. While I am trying to get in, someone else goes down ahead of me."**

To Jesus' question, the man gave reasons as to why he couldn't get well. The answer was, "Yes, I want to get well if only..." If only he had a friend, then he could get to the waters. What are your "if only" statements?

Perhaps you've said, "If only my father wasn't a drunk," "If only I hadn't been abused as a child," "If only my husband hadn't left me," "If only my child didn't die," "If only

I had gotten a degree," "If only I lived in the right neighbor-hood," etc. What have you zeroed in on as the reason why you are not further ahead?

Jesus ignored the limitations of the man's "if only" state-ments. He wanted to transition the man to the world of "even if." Even if he had no friend to take him to the pool when the waters were stirred, Jesus is all He needed. What about you? What are your "Even if" statements? Even if a loved one is diagnosed with an illness, Jesus is all you need to get through the crisis. Even if you lose your job, Jesus will get you through your time of unemployment. Even if the person who promised to love you forever walks out, Jesus will put someone else in your life or meet the need Himself.

God won't be boxed in by our solutions and lack of imagination. The man had been lying in the same place a long time. Perhaps he once had friends who began with him. But since no one knew the timing of when the water would be stirred, whoever began with him no longer waited. Jesus found the man at a time when he assessed himself in John 5:7a as having "no one to help me into the pool." He had no friend left. Have you ever been in a place where you felt en-tirely alone?

The good news with having no friend left is that you're also in a place where no one else is offering you a solu-tion. When we first encounter challenges, there are times when we have so many opinions coming our way that we are inundated with information. The more information and opinions that come our way, the more confused we can become. The lame man was in a place where the opin-ions had stopped. No one even cared any more to offer one.

Then, out of nowhere, a stranger stood in front of him, offering an answer.

There are times God lets us stay in a place with no answers before He decides to show up. The man was ready for anyone to show interest. He was ready for any answer. More than that, he was ready to listen to this one opinion because it was the only opinion after a time of silence.

I don't know about you, but I'm tired of people who don't stand by what they say. It's like they have to hedge every statement because they can't assure you of anything. Oh, the breath of fresh air to hear God offer a solution with authority, interest in you, and confidence in the answer!

John 5:8–9a reads: **Then Jesus said to him, "Get up! Pick up your mat and walk." At once the man was cured; he picked up his mat and walked.**

Jesus told the man to "Get up!" In the same breath, Jesus added, "Pick up your mat and walk." Imagine the invalid who had been lying there in a crippled state for thirty-eight years. The idea of getting up must have sounded overwhelming. Before he could even adjust to the first idea, Jesus wasted no time in saying, "Pick up your mat." Then without a pause, the sentence rolled into, "Pick up your mat and walk."

God is not into half-baked solutions. God may choose to work in stages, but He isn't limited to them. When God created the world out of nothing, He said in Genesis 1:3, **"Let there be light,"** and there was light. There wasn't partial light that grew into full light; there was instant light. With one thought, with one word, God's will is done! Have you ever questioned God's power to heal completely?

Right after Jesus' commands, John 5:9 tells us that "at once" the man was cured. His healing occurred as soon as Jesus spoke. It was after he was cured that **"he picked up his mat and walked."**

In the story of the invalid, God chose to act independently of the invalid's faith. God's act of mercy wasn't dependent on the man's belief but on the man's desire. God didn't say, "Do you believe in me?" He didn't say, "Do you believe in yourself to walk again?" He said, "Do you want to get well?"

In God's mercy, His words released the power in the man's body. John 5:9 tells us that "at once" the man experienced his cure. It was after he felt the cure in his body that he knew he could obey the command to pick up his mat and walk. His was not the situation of trying to get up, or trying to walk before experiencing the strength. His was not a situation of having the faith first before he could walk. His was a situation of experiencing the cure and then going and living the reality of the cure.

Do you lack faith for yourself? If you don't have faith for God's provision because you don't feel worthy, then have faith in God's character to show mercy. Have faith that God will reveal His power when it fits His bigger mission.

My application

God heals us because it fits His mission to reveal the Messiah as healer. I remember when God healed my son of asthma. I kept warning him to take his medicine with him. He kept saying he didn't need it. I insisted that, medically, asthma is a permanent condition. I also remembered stories of how God healed someone but the illness came back. My son was being flippant and needed to be more serious about his condition. I, on the other hand, needed to relax and trust God's purpose as healer. God's healing, whether permanent or temporary, tells us something about God's power. God may decide to grant healing for a season or for a lifetime. The ultimate goal then is not the healing but what God reveals about Himself.

I recall a time my two dogs got lost. When I drove around to look for them, I found them darting back and forth in the middle of the road. All traffic was stopped waiting them to decide which way they were going. I shouted their names and they immediately stood frozen. Then they ran as fast as they could towards my car. When they jumped in the car, they were panting but I could tell they were relieved. Before I rescued them, they had known me as the one who fed them. But that day, they also knew me as their protector. Those dogs bonded with me in a more intimate way because I had rescued them. In a similar way, when God reveals Himself as healer, He does so to show us more of Himself. Whether God heals me permanently or temporarily, He reveals His power as Messiah.

YOUR APPLICATION

Imagine a person with an illness who experienced healing. Now imagine the illness flaring up again. Share how you responded to the reoccurrence of the illness. What if it fit God's purpose for the healing to be temporary? Share what purpose God could have accomplished by granting someone temporary health and giving them additional time on earth.

DAY 1

Devotion

IN GOD'S MASTER PLAN, HE

INCLUDES THE MIRACULOUS—

DON'T MISS OUT ON RECEIVING

THE MIRACLE THAT FULFILLS

GOD'S MISSION.

G OD'S ACTS OF MERCY ARE INFLUENCED BY HIS PUR-
pose. The Book of John was written to show readers
that Jesus was the Messiah. So, the Apostle John tells us the
story of Jesus walking into Jerusalem and singling out an
invalid to bless. Healing a lame man was consistent with
God's purpose.

Zephaniah 3:14–20 tells us: **Sing, O Daughter of Zion;
shout aloud, O Israel! …The LORD, the King of Israel,
is with you; never again will you fear any harm…At that
time I will deal with all who oppressed you;** I will rescue

the lame **and gather those who have been scattered.** (Underline added for emphasis.)

In Zephaniah 3:14, did you see the verb "sing?" Did you see the words "shout aloud?" God delights in doing things that evoke our celebration. He loves filling us with wonderment over His greatness. In fulfilling one of His roles as Messiah, Jesus was ready to heal a lame man who had been in that position for a long time.

Think of yourself walking down the halls of a hospital with patients everywhere who have a terminal illness. When you and I walk down those halls, the feeling of helplessness can throw anyone into depression. Now, imagine God walking down that hall. He comes unannounced. He walks by one hospital room, then the next. For reasons He does not disclose to anyone, He stops at a room and focuses on one patient. He asks the question as He did in John 5:6b, **"Do you want to get well?"**

Imagine there were no family members around to answer the question or to insist on what God must do. There was no nurse around. There was only the person who had endured suffering for many years face-to-face with the great physician. What comforts my heart is to realize that God lives on an eternal timeline. He doesn't see healing as confined to our time and space. To God, healing someone by taking them into eternity is as much a healing as restoring someone's health while on earth. To the question, "Do you want to get well?" God then chooses the kind of healing He will offer. God will choose in a way that aligns with His purpose. Before we were born, He already ordained the number of days we will have on earth. Job 14:5 tells us,

"Man's days are determined; you have decreed the number of his months and have set limits he cannot exceed."

Healing the lame man fit God's purpose. Our Redeemer still lives today. God's heart is still to reveal His Son to the world as Messiah. Are you ready to ask Him to use your life to showcase His mercy? Will you trust that whatever God chooses to do is an act of mercy?

MY APPLICATION

Like the lame man, I had been struggling for so long in the losses of my life that I finally reconciled myself to my losses. I no longer lived with the expectation that life could be different. I simply accepted the pattern of abandonment. Why is it that my mother who dreamed of my future didn't live to see it? Why is it that God repeated the pattern in a spiritual father who was diagnosed with Alzheimer's disease? I knew the statistics on people with dementia or Alzheimer's. It wasn't like God singled him out for some rare disease. God simply allowed him to be a statistic among others who are also suffering. I so wanted God to mark him as one destined for a miracle. In the same way Jesus stopped for the invalid who had been crippled for thirty-eight years, why didn't Jesus stop for the friend I wanted to keep in my life? I just knew that I would walk in one day and he would have his mind completely restored. Jesus could do that so easily.

Instead, the disease weakened my friend on a daily basis. And then the most incredible thing happened. God redirected my attention to the greater miracle.

The miracle of healing was taking place in the hearts of those entrusted with the care of a loved one. In our physical eyes, what we see is someone's physical disability. What God sees is the disability in our hearts. Without realizing it, we're all cripples when it comes to loving others. Could it be that God allows certain illnesses that require extravagant love as His way to give us a chance to love extravagantly? The real miracle is the transformation in the hearts of those who love unconditionally. It takes unconditional love to keep loving someone who is unable to recognize you or love you back. I had appealed to God's mercy to bring about physical healing of a friend. God chose to demonstrate mercy by transforming my crippled heart to keep on loving even when a friend couldn't love me back.

YOUR APPLICATION

Describe a time you or a loved one was a statistic in a bad situation. Share whether you expected God to show you mercy. If God were to pick one person to heal, share whether you would want God to heal you or if you would ask God to heal someone else. How does your choice show your trust or lack of trust in God's purpose?

DAY 2

Devotion

EVEN WHEN GOD'S ACTIVITY IS

OBVIOUS, SOME STILL MISS IT—

YOU WON'T SEE GOD WORK IF

YOU'RE TOO OCCUPIED WITH

CRITICIZING HIM.

———

JOHN 5:9B-10 READS: **The day on which this took place was a Sabbath, and so the Jews said to the man who had been healed, "It is the Sabbath; the law forbids you to carry your mat."**

In John 5:10, the Jews said to the man who had been healed, **"the law forbids you to carry your mat."** They totally overlooked the fact that the man was healed and zeroed in on finding fault.

Let's look at why the Jewish leaders criticized the work Jesus did on the Sabbath. What exactly was the controversy?

To understand the significance, we need to understand the origins of the Sabbath.

The first mention of the word "Sabbath" was when God gave Moses and His chosen people manna in the desert. He rained down manna for six days. On the sixth day, he rained down twice the supply and commanded the people to rest on the seventh day.

Exodus 16:29–30 reads: **"Bear in mind that the LORD has given you the Sabbath; that is why on the sixth day he gives you bread for two days. Everyone is to stay where he is on the seventh day; no one is to go out." So the people rested on the seventh day.**

The Sabbath is a rest day modeled after God's work pattern when He first created the world. The International Standard Encyclopedia said, "The Sabbath was meant to be a blessing to man and not a burden. Even those who were servants were required to rest on the Sabbath."

Exodus 31:12–17 reads: **Then the LORD said to Moses, "Say to the Israelites, 'You must observe my Sabbaths. This will be a sign between me and you for the generations to come, so you may know that I am the LORD, who makes you holy...The Israelites are to observe the Sabbath, celebrating it for the generations to come as a lasting covenant. It will be a sign between me and the Israelites forever, for in six days the LORD made the heavens and the earth, and on the seventh day he abstained from work and rested.'"**

God described the Sabbath as a lasting covenant. According to Nelson's Illustrated Bible Dictionary, "A covenant, in the biblical sense, implies much more than a contract or simple agreement. A contract always has an end date, while a covenant is a permanent arrangement."

The Sabbath was designed to identify who God is and who God's people are! The Sabbath was created as a lasting covenant between God and His people. It was a sign that set God's people apart from the general public.

Deuteronomy 5:15 reads: **Remember that you were slaves in Egypt and that the LORD your God brought you out of there with a mighty hand and an outstretched arm. Therefore the LORD your God has commanded you to observe the Sabbath day.**

The Sabbath was also a reminder of God's protection and salvation. He stretched out His hand to part the Red Sea and saved the people from the Egyptian army.

Jesus worked on the Sabbath because the Sabbath was meant to represent a special relationship between God and His people. The Sabbath was intended to be a blessing, not a hardship. So, here on the Sabbath, God chose to bless the lame man.

The Jewish leaders criticized Jesus for healing the lame man. By focusing on criticizing God's activity, have you missed out on what God wants to reveal about Himself?

MY APPLICATION

Jesus worked on the Sabbath because God intended the Sabbath to be a blessing. Those who criticize Jesus were not connected with God's heart. I've met people who measure spirituality based on whether or not you go to church. It matters little what else you do the rest of the time. The test of spirituality becomes whether or not you show up on Sunday. They put guilt trips on others when they can't go to church, even if they are ill or physically exhausted. Although God wants us to worship Him and not to forsake the fellowship of believers, God doesn't want us to live according to a checklist of do's and don'ts. He wants us to desire to be set apart from the world. He wants us to do things that set us apart because we are proud to be counted among His holy people. Whenever I do things because I have to, I need to check my motives. We will burn out doing things out of obligation. It's only when we serve out of the heart of a son or daughter who wants to be part of God's family that we serve with joy.

Your application

Describe a time you totally ignored the results and criticized a process or a person. Share how you missed out on celebrating the miraculous by allowing a critical spirit to dominate your life.

DAY 3

WHEN GOD INTERVENES IN

OUR LIFE, HE EXPECTS OUR

FUTURE TO CHANGE—HAVE YOU

FORGOTTEN GOD BY RETURNING

TO LIFE AS IT USED TO BE?

———◆———

HAS GOD TOUCHED YOUR LIFE IN SOME WAY? HOW have you changed your priorities since God intervened in your life?

John 5:14–15 reads: **Later Jesus found him at the temple and said to him, "See, you are well again. Stop sinning or something worse may happen to you." The man went away and told the Jews that it was Jesus who had made him well.**

Since Jesus found the healed man at the temple, this tells us he was grateful to God. He went to the temple to praise God for his healing. It was there that Jesus found him.

In John 5:14b, when Jesus said, **"Stop sinning or something worse may happen to you,"** this tells us the invalid's handicap was a punishment for sin. This doesn't mean that every disabled person's handicap is a result of sin. For example, God's Word tells us about the healing of a blind man. When the disciples asked Jesus if his blindness was caused by sin, Jesus said in John 9:3: **"Neither this man nor his parents sinned," said Jesus, "but this happened so that the work of God might be displayed in his life."** However, in the case of this invalid, God said it was the result of sin.

Matthew Henry said in his commentary in *PC Study Bible Version 5*, "whether of some remarkably flagrant sin, or only of sin in general, we cannot tell, but we know that sin is the procuring cause of sickness,

Psalms 107:17–19 reads: **Some became fools through their rebellious ways and suffered affliction because of their iniquities. They loathed all food and drew near the gates of death. Then they cried to the LORD in their trouble, and he saved them from their distress."**

Has God ever allowed a handicap in your life to redirect your attention to Him? Whether our condition was a result of our own sin or otherwise, God wants us to honor Him in our health and suffering. Therefore, Jesus warns the man, "or something worse may happen to you."

God has the power to completely heal us. At the same time, He also has the power to remove His hands of protection. It offends God when we forget about Him after He has healed us. When God has shown us that we cannot function without His grace, He expects us to realize that our life belongs to Him. Any strength we have is a result of His provision. Any great ideas we have in ministry or business are a result of His provision. To continue in health without offering God our lives to serve Him is an offense. It's like saying to God, "Now that I got what I wanted, I don't need you anymore!"

My application

When God heals us, He expects us to remember our deliverance. However, He doesn't want us to serve Him out of obligation, but out of relationship. Years ago, I was in a horrific car accident. When I realized God saved me from being killed, I was filled with praise. Then, over time, I forgot how bad things could've been, and my appreciation began to wane. I forgot my commitment to serve God with my life. God allowed me to enter a time of depression as His way to remind me that He owned my life. It was in this depression that I remembered my divine encounter and how I had strayed from God. I immediately repented and asked God to give me another chance to commit my life to His purpose.

YOUR APPLICATION

Describe a time God delivered you from illness or a bad situation. Share how your priorities changed as a result of your deliverance or share how you forgot about God's deliverance over time and went back to life as it used to be.

DAY 4
Devotion

GOD SHARES HIS PLANS WITH

THOSE HE CAN TRUST—ARE

YOU CLOSE ENOUGH A FRIEND

FOR GOD TO TRUST YOU WITH

MORE DETAILS?

——————

JOHN 5:16–18 READS: **So, because Jesus was doing these things on the Sabbath, the Jews persecuted him. Jesus said to them, "My Father is always at his work to this very day, and I, too, am working." For this reason the Jews tried all the harder to kill him; not only was he breaking the Sabbath, but he was even calling God his own Father, making himself equal with God.**

Jesus was God. Because of this, He was being true to His character in showing mercy to an invalid. Because the Jewish leaders didn't believe Jesus was God, his activity was an insult to the Sabbath. So, Jesus made it blatant that He was God by saying in John 5:17a, "My Father is always at his work." He was saying, "God intends to be a blessing, even on a Sabbath!" This made the Jewish leaders even madder. In John 5:18a, they tried "the harder to kill him." In their minds, they were being spiritual. They thought they were protecting God's reputation.

In John 5:19, Jesus reiterates that He is the Father's son. He said, "I tell you the truth, the Son can do nothing by himself; he can do only what he sees his Father doing, because whatever the Father does the Son also does." Not only did Jesus heal on Sabbath, He was saying that the Father would have done the same thing. He does nothing except what the Father does.

John 5:20–21 reads: For the Father loves the Son and shows him all he does. Yes, to your amazement he will show him even greater things than these. For just as the Father raises the dead and gives them life, even so the Son gives life to whom he is pleased to give it.

Jesus explains why the Son is in tune with what the Father is doing. According to John 5:20a, Jesus says it is because the "Father loves the Son" that He "shows him all he does." Jesus tells the Jewish leader that the reason the Son knows what the Father is doing is because of love and relationship. In those statements, He was also accusing them of missing what the Father was doing because they lacked relationship.

Have you ever seen a plumber teach his son about plumbing? Have you watched a mother teach her child how to cook? One way we demonstrate love to our children is to pass down to them what we know. God loved Jesus and didn't hide anything from Him. Jesus is fully aware of all that the Father is doing.

On the flipside, it's hard to feel loved when you are around those who hide what they are doing. Do you have trouble feeling loved by a spouse who won't show you the finances and leaves you wondering if you will have enough to live on? Do you have trouble trusting a boss who won't share the future plans of the company or what he or she is working on as priorities? Relationships are built through transparency. The Father didn't only show Jesus some of what he did. John 5:20a tells us God showed Jesus "all he does." (Underline added for emphasis.)

If I don't know God's plans, is it because I haven't loved God enough? Is God withholding His revelation because He doesn't trust my love for Him and His plans? In John 5:21, Jesus elaborates on a relationship where God not only shows the Son what He is doing but also empowers the Son. God has given authority to His Son to judge all men, including these Jewish leaders!

John 5:22–23a reads: **Moreover, the Father judges no one, but has entrusted all judgment to the Son, that all may honor the Son just as they honor the Father.**

As God reveals the truth of Jesus to the world, Jesus isn't bashful in defending God's message. While the leaders were adamant that Jesus wasn't God, Jesus continues in John 5:22, beginning with the word "Moreover." He was putting more fuel on the fire to their rage. While the Jewish leaders were judging Jesus, He was saying that He alone was given the authority to judge. In other words, He had the power to judge them, to convict them, and to sentence them. His sentence could keep them from eternal life and fellowship with God.

Can you imagine continuing with these statements with an audience that already expressed they didn't believe Jesus was God? By Jesus' example, we learn that God does not tiptoe around the truth. He expects those who love Him to defend His truth. Jesus didn't say, "Let them warm up to the idea that I am God first before telling them more." He didn't hesitate to say "Moreover" and to continue with the implications, given that Jesus is God. Saying "Moreover" is saying "And one more thing..."

In defiance of the odds against you or those who attack you, are you that sure of God's message that you can say, "And one more thing"? "Jesus has risen from the dead. And one more thing, He is alive and seated at the right hand of the Father. And one more thing, all authority in heaven and earth belongs to Him. And one more thing, He is the chief judge and He judges me as righteous. And one more thing, the power with which God raised Jesus is available to me in my life."

Jesus loved God and defended God's truth. God didn't hesitate to reveal "all" things to the One He could trust with His message. What about you? How much can God trust you to love Him and to defend His message? If you find yourself in the dark over God's plans, could it be because you haven't demonstrated trustworthiness to justify hearing more of God's plans?

MY APPLICATION

God revealed all things to Jesus because Jesus was one with the Father in heart and mission. God told Jesus everything because God could trust Him. As a young believer, I was frustrated because God was often silent when I asked Him to reveal His will to me. I felt like all I was doing was studying God's Word, with no specific assignment or mission. I realize now that God was using my time of preparation to see if I would remain faithful to Him. God was seeing if He could trust me!

I was in Beth Moore's Sunday School class for seven years. At the same time, I was in Bible Study Fellowship for six years. Then I enrolled at Dallas Theological Seminary. Because I was working full time, I pursued my studies at Dallas Theological Seminary on a part-time basis and took seven years to graduate. Looking back, I think it's more challenging to stay disciplined for seven years of study than to rush through an accelerated program in two years! Through all that time, God seemed silent. Then, the month I graduated from Dallas Theological Seminary in 2003, God led me to establish the ministry of Inspire Women. It was like I turned the corner and all of a sudden God was downloading marching orders on a daily basis. What God has taught me over the years is that He speaks most when I am fully surrendered. So, when I don't hear God, I first ask myself, "Is there something I have done that has caused God not to trust me anymore?"

Your application

Describe a time God grew silent in your life. Share whether your choices influenced God's silence. If so, what must you change to regain God's trust? If you don't discern any legitimate reason for God's silence, share whether the ball is in your court and if God's silence is because He hasn't changed His original marching orders. In other words, what did you last hear God say and have you obeyed?

DAY 5
Devotion

WHEN WE KEEP ASKING FOR

SIGNS, WE KEEP OURSELVES FROM

BEING FULLY COMMITTED—

CONFIRM YOUR CALLING BY

FINISHING YOUR MISSION.

JOHN 5:28–30 READS: **"Do not be amazed at this, for a time is coming when all who are in their graves will hear his voice and come out—those who have done good will rise to live, and those who have done evil will rise to be condemned. By myself I can do nothing; I judge only as I hear, and my judgment is just, for I seek not to please myself but him who sent me."**

Jesus says, **"Do not be amazed"** because He observed the amazed looks on the faces of the audience. First of all, they did not believe He was God. Then, to think He had authority to judge them pushed them over the edge. So, Jesus tells them not to be amazed and speaks of a future when all who are in the grave will hear His voice. He then reiterates that His power to raise the dead is a power bestowed upon Him by God the Father. Even in His acts of power, it isn't because He's on any kind of power trip. Instead, according to John 5:30b, He uses His power in alignment with God's purpose and He lives **"not to please myself but him who sent me."**

Has God ever entrusted you with power? How have you used this power to please God as compared to getting the approval of fallen humanity? One of the ways we can please God is to finish what He sent us to do.

John 5:36 reads: **"For the very work that the Father has given me to finish, and which I am doing, testifies that the Father has sent me."**

In John 5:36, Jesus tells us that His proof that the Father sent Him is evidenced in his ability to "finish." In the midst of the persecution or hardship, one way to confirm your calling is to ask God for the power to finish your mission. Instead of trying to defend yourself, stay focused on what God has given you to do. Keep working towards what God trusted you to do. Know from Jesus' example that God always finishes. And when you finish the work God sent you to do, all who criticized you or were suspicious of your motives will know that God sent you.

MY APPLICATION

Jesus said His proof that the Father sent Him was by finishing what the Father sent Him to do. When I first started Inspire Women, I was sure God wanted a ministry to release the full potential of women of all ethnicities and economic levels to complete God's spiritual army for missions and ministry. There were key leaders in the city who frowned on my efforts because they didn't believe God would trust women in leadership roles in ministry.

Inspire Women was unique in that the ministry not only inspired women to live God's purpose but also provided empowerment through scholarships for biblical training, mentoring of shepherd/leaders, and the funding of ministry grants to empower women to serve. Most women's ministries did not have a large budget to invest in the training of women or the funding of resources. The critics accused me of being misinformed. Their thinking was, "If you have a dollar to spend, you should invest in the men because they have more impact." One wise pastor told me to stop listening to the criticism and to just focus on the work. He then offered me this counsel, "When they see what God will do through you, they will support you." He was speaking what God had already shown me in the life of Jesus. The way to evidence God's call in my life is to finish God's call for my life. Instead of focusing on the naysayers, I must always choose to focus on completing the work. God cannot confirm His calling through half-finished assignments.

Your application

Describe something God put on your heart to do. Share the challenges you encountered along the way and whether or not you have finished. Share whether you have been asking God for more signs to confirm your calling. Say whether your appeal for more signs could be an act of procrastination to avoid a difficult assignment.

WEEKEND
Reflection

MY APPLICATION

My spiritual mother used to be in God's Word all the time and enjoyed her prayer times. I now see my confidante sitting and staring at the ceiling. The question I was struggling with was this: Where is God? Does she still have a relationship with God when her brain is not able to process information? Then one day, God settled my question through His Word.

Psalms 139:13–16 reads: **For you created my inmost being; you knit me together in my mother's womb. I praise you because I am fearfully and wonderfully made; your works are wonderful, I know that full well. My frame was not hidden from you when I was made in the secret place.**

When I was woven together in the depths of the earth, your eyes saw my unformed body. All the days ordained for me were written in your book before one of them came to be.

God taught me that as a fetus in our mother's womb or even in the early days of our existence on earth, we weren't cognizant of God's care.

Yet His Word tells us He was there. More than just being there, He also ordained all the days of our lives.

He isn't surprised by a season of hardship or illness. He designs the kind of worship He wants from each life, whether that worship comes in the form of our success or in the cross He chooses for us to carry.

I believe a biblical perspective is to view old age, dementia, or Alzheimer's

like returning to life as when it first began. During the first sign of life in us in our mother's womb and during our first days on earth, God was with us, though we were not aware of it. Therefore, in a stage of life when our brain cells may no longer register information as it used to, I know God is there, though our bodies may not be as aware of our surroundings.

The great news is, a most remarkable thing is about to happen. When we first became aware of God on earth, we experienced a new birth and an awakening to a reality we were oblivious to. We experienced euphoria and celebration in receiving the gift of eternal life through Jesus. In old age, dementia, or Alzheimer's we know what our future holds. Life may get harder for a little while, but then things will totally turn around. We will experience a different awakening beyond any we have experienced on earth. When the time comes for us to step into the arms of our heavenly Father in eternity, we will see and hear clearer than ever before. All tears will be dried and all things will be made new. Best of all, we will have full knowledge: We will be fully aware of the acts of kindness and pure extravagant love from family and friends that was poured out to us.

In the same way Jesus stopped to address the need of a cripple of thirty eight years, I knew God looked my way to settle my question. I will never know why God chose to show me mercy. I just know He did and I am truly grateful.

Your application

Describe a situation you have wrestled with for many years. Perhaps you carry emotional or physical scars from a childhood experience. Perhaps you have experienced a nasty divorce. Perhaps you have lost a child, and the grief continues to overwhelm you. Describe the lingering pain and longings in your heart. Then describe your response to Jesus' question, "Do you want to get well?" Share any insight or comfort this chapter gave you.

7

Trust God to provide for His dreams

"Just when the caterpillar thought the world
was over, it became a butterfly."

Anonymous

WHETHER YOU ARE BUILDING a business, a family, or a ministry, you've probably faced a situation of lacking the required resources to reach your goals. While wrestling with a lack of resources, don't expect life to stand still to give you time to figure things out. In the midst of trying to make ends meet, expect the dishwasher to break down, the kids to be fighting, or a friend to misunderstand your intentions and get mad at you. I have found that when emotional tension is high, this is when I am hit with more drama that escalates the tension. Have you ever said, "What's going on? If one more bad thing happens, I think I'm going to break!"

As if the tension isn't enough, while trying to solve the problem, I often hear the voice of the critics. It seems that everyone has a different idea about how to solve the problem, though no one is responsible for whether or not their idea will work. It's so much easier to be a commentator than to take ownership for results. Does it make you mad to hear people say, "That wasn't handled well" or "That's not the way I would have done it?" Don't you want to say, "Then why don't *you* do it?" Of course, they don't want to own the problem, they just want to talk about it and talk about you!

In this situation, what are we to do? Is there something in your life you've left undone because of a lack of resources? Did you know that God wants us to see that life isn't a mission of "Me against the world?" Rather, God wants us to operate under the banner of "God and me against the challenges of the world." In fact, in your darkest moments, the journey of "God and me against the challenges of the world" will carry us to a place where God will teach us how to fly!

When you are walking with God, the idea of scarce resources is an opposite concept to His sufficiency. How could we lack anything when God is walking with us? Jesus tells us in Matthew 6:25–27, **"Therefore I tell you, do not worry about your life, what you will eat or drink; or about your body, what you will wear. Is not life more important than food, and the body more important than clothes? Look at the birds of the air; they do not sow or reap or store away in barns, and yet your heavenly**

Father feeds them. Are you not much more valuable than they? Who of you by worrying can add a single hour to his life?

Jesus says in Matthew 6:31–33, **"So do not worry, saying, 'What shall we eat?' or 'What shall we drink?' or 'What shall we wear?' For the pagans run after all these things, and your heavenly Father knows that you need them. But seek first his kingdom and his righteousness, and all these things will be given to you as well."**

In Matthew 6:33, God's Word tells us that when we **"seek first his kingdom and his righteousness"** then **"all these things will be given to you as well."** If you're staring at scarcity while seeking God's will, trust God to provide. God is practical. Matthew 6:32b tells us that **"your heavenly Father knows that you need them."** I've heard some zealous servants of God say, "I will starve if I need to in order to serve God!" I think there are times some Christians offer to be martyrs when God hasn't called them to that sacrifice. It isn't necessary to starve when we can trust God for His provision! It's one thing if you are serving God in a third world country where no one has any resources. But it makes no sense to starve when we are serving while surrounded by believers blessed with prosperity and financial strength!

In John 6, we will read the story of the disciples faced with a lack of resources to fulfill God's plans. They were next to God and given a directive from Him to provide food for the crowd. That's like someone standing next to the biggest billionaire in the city and being told to hand out money to some local poor. Yet we will see how our own lack of expectation can limit us. Let's learn from how Jesus dealt with the disciples' lack of faith.

John 6:1–2 reads: **Some time after this, Jesus crossed to the far shore of the Sea of Galilee (that is, the Sea of Tiberias), and a great crowd of people followed him because they saw the miraculous signs he had performed on the sick.**

John 6:1a begins with the words **"Some time after this."** I find myself inquiring, "Some time after what?" It was after the healing of the invalid who had been a cripple for thirty-eight years that the story continues. It was after the Jewish leaders argued with Jesus and accused Him of breaking the law by healing a man on the Sabbath that we see Jesus getting into a boat to cross to the far shore of the Sea of Galilee. In the midst of the controversy between Jesus and the Jewish leaders, John 6:2a tells us there was **"a great crowd of people"** who witnessed the miracle. Have you ever been in a place where you did not fully understand what was going on but knew something miraculous had happened?

God doesn't ever want us to be so caught up by the details of a controversy that we miss the bigger picture of what He is doing. John 6:2 tells us that a great crowd of people followed Jesus **"because they saw the miraculous signs he had performed."** A great crowd followed Jesus because they witnessed the miracles He performed on the sick.

John 6:3–4 reads: **Then Jesus went up on a mountainside and sat down with his disciples. The Jewish Passover Feast was near.**

The Apostle John gives us an idea of what was happening in the community. He tells us in John 6:4 that this was the time when **"The Jewish Passover Feast was near."** What is spiritually significant about the Jewish Passover?

If someone tells you it's the Christmas season and you have no idea what Christmas is about, any meaning will be lost on you. But if you understood what normally happens during the Christmas season, you would know that people will probably be rushing around, getting their house ready, buying presents, mailing out Christmas cards, and generally preparing for a time of celebration. If you were in tune to the spirit of Christmas, you would know the Christmas season is probably not the right time to advertise a financial seminar on saving money when most people's minds are on buying gifts.

When God's Word tells us the Jewish Passover was near, it should alert us to the fact that the community was focused on celebrating God's provision. The Passover commemorated the time when the angel of wrath killed the firstborn of the Egyptians but passed over the houses of the Jewish people. The houses marked by the blood of a sacrificial lamb were spared.

God is the master storyteller. So, here we have Jesus, the lamb who will be sacrificed for the people, walking onto the scene during the time of the "Jewish Passover Feast." The dramatic tension is from this question: During the celebration of God's provision, how will the lamb of God, personified by Jesus, provide for the hungry people?

Are you in tune to the story that is unfolding around you? What season do you find yourself in? Have you ever missed God's story by missing the significance of what is happening around you?

John 6:5–6 reads: **When Jesus looked up and saw a great crowd coming toward him, he said to Philip,**

"Where shall we buy bread for these people to eat?" He asked this only to test him, for he already had in mind what he was going to do.

The Book of John was written so we would know that Jesus is the Christ. As the Christ, Jesus was the greater Moses. In the Old Testament, Moses asked God for provision, and God rained down manna from heaven. In the New Testament, God wanted the people to see that Jesus was the bread of life. To drive home this point, Jesus began by feeding the people with physical bread before instructing them about the spiritual bread that leads to eternal life. In His plans to take care of the people, Jesus asked Philip, "Where shall we buy bread for these people to eat?" (Underline added for emphasis.)

Philip immediately started figuring out how to solve the problem. He totally missed the fact that Jesus said, "Where shall we buy bread?" Jesus didn't say, "Where will you buy bread?" God wasn't challenging Philip to come up with an answer. He already had the answer. We know this because John 6:6 stated, "**He asked this only to test him, for he already had in mind what he was going to do.**"

So, what was the test? The test was in whether Philip recognized Jesus as the bread of life who would feed the people not only physical bread but spiritual bread. What about you? Do you recognize Jesus as the breazd that will give you eternal life? If you can trust God for eternity, how much more can you trust God for your every day needs!

John 6:7 reads: **Philip answered him, "Eight months' wages would not buy enough bread for each one to have a bite!"**

Phillip flunked the test. He totally missed the fact that God wanted him to recognize Jesus as the Messiah and trust the Messiah to provide. What about you? When you are faced with a need, do you immediately feel the weight of the world on your shoulders? How do you assess if the need in front of you is a need God wants to meet? Who are "these people" Jesus referred to in John 6:5? It was the crowd that was following Jesus. Did you know that when you are faced with a need when following Jesus, God makes the need His problem to solve? Therefore, have the confidence God will show you how to meet the need.

Phillip missed the fact that Jesus was the Messiah and that the Messiah will save those who seek Him. So, he assessed the hunger situation with his mental power and tried to solve the problem. He did the math in his head and concluded in John 6:7 that **"Eight months' wages would not buy enough bread for each one to have a bite!"**

Are you guilty of shutting down God's plans with your math? Just imagine Jesus standing next to you with His vision to feed the people. Jesus was perfectly confident that He was the bread of life. Because He was the bread of life, He had the capacity to feed every single person who came to Him. To show them His power to provide for everyone, He was now going to feed the entire crowd physically.

There are times God will deliver us physically as evidence that He can deliver us spiritually. For example, look at the healing of the paralytic. Jesus healed the paralytic to evidence His greater power to forgive sins. But since we can't see with our physical eyes whether sin is forgiven, Jesus demonstrates His power by an outward healing.

Luke 5:22–26 reads: **Jesus knew what they were thinking and asked, "Why are you thinking these things in your hearts? Which is easier: to say, 'Your sins are forgiven,' or to say, 'Get up and walk?' But that you may know that the Son of Man has authority on earth to forgive sins. . ." He said to the paralyzed man, "I tell you, get up, take your mat and go home." Immediately he stood up in front of them, took what he had been lying on and went home praising God. Everyone was amazed and gave praise to God. They were filled with awe and said, "We have seen remarkable things today."**

Jesus invited Philip to join Him in an event to prove to the crowds that He was the Messiah, the bread of life. Philip totally missed God's ultimate goal. In the needs you struggle with, has it ever occurred to you that your need is the perfect setting for God to show off who He is? Meeting the need serves a greater purpose than just meeting your need. Have you jettisoned God's plan by intervening to solve the problem your way?

John 6:8–9 reads: **Another of his disciples, Andrew, Simon Peter's brother, spoke up, "Here is a boy with five small barley loaves and two small fish, but how far will they go among so many?"**

At least Andrew didn't just do the math in his head. He actually took the time to look for resources. Perhaps you took the time to look in every bank account. You took the time to see what stocks you could sell. You took the time to see if you could get a second mortgage on the house. At least you did your homework and, in your mind, tried to make things work. However, like Andrew, did you find yourself concluding as stated in John 6:9, "Here is a boy with five small barley loaves and two small fish, but how far will they go among so many?"

In John 6:9, Andrew said "small" barley loaves. He said "small" fish. He made sure God knew how small the resources were. Have you ever said to God, "Here is my small savings!" or "Here is my small paycheck?"

When my brother came to this country, my mother sold all she had to buy him a one-way ticket. He knew his money would run out in six months. Yet, he had the courage to embark on a journey into the unknown. He took the risk for a better physical and financial future. Instead of staring at the "small" amount of money in his hands, he focused on a big future. Meanwhile, my mother covered him in prayer every day. God opened doors for my brother. When he graduated, he started out at IBM and advanced to a senior level. Today, he's a retired senior vice president of Fidelity Investments. It was while he was in this country that he met my sister-in-law. She was a Christian and she led him to Christ. Just imagine what would have been lost had he not stepped out in faith with my mother's small savings.

Is there something you have left undone because you allowed the scarcity of resource to frighten you?

My application

When God called me to start Inspire Women, I had to make the decision to leave an established institution. I had no money in the bank. I had just one person on staff, and no idea how to pay her. Instead of staring at my small bank account, I looked across the city and saw thousands of women across ethnicities and economic levels whose lives were disconnected from God. I knew God wanted to mobilize His entire spiritual army to live for Him. I understood I was in the middle of a God-sized mission. I learned it was perfectly fine to state the facts. In the same way, it would have been fine if Andrew had said, "Here is a boy with five small barley loaves and two small fish" and stopped there. His would have been a statement of fact. What wasn't fine was when he continued with the words "but how far will they go among so many?" Instead of leaving the facts with God, Andrew went into evaluation mode and allowed the facts to be bigger than God.

What God taught me was to know the facts. Faith shouldn't be because I'm clueless to the severity or urgency of the problem. Faith is knowing your resource cannot meet the need, and then trusting that the question "Where shall we buy bread?" means God is part of the "we" who will find bread. More than that, God is the dominant "we." He will lead and I will follow. The question to God's question, "Where shall we buy bread?" should be "Wherever you want to buy bread, Lord."

YOUR APPLICATION

Describe a situation where you lacked the resources to reach your goal. Share who you asked and where you looked to count your resources. Now write down some possibilities you didn't consider because they were outside your comfort zone. Which do you think is God's solution?

Day 1

GOD WILL NOT INVITE YOU TO
PARTICIPATE IF YOU DON'T TRUST
HIS VISION—HAS YOUR LACK OF
EXPECTATION KEPT YOU FROM
BEING INCLUDED?

—◆—

JOHN 6:10–11 READS: **Jesus said, "Have the people sit down." There was plenty of grass in that place, and the men sat down, about five thousand of them. Jesus then took the loaves, gave thanks, and distributed to those who were seated as much as they wanted. He did the same with the fish.**

Observe that Jesus didn't argue with the disciples over whether they had enough resources to feed the people. There are times when people who are stuck in their logic need to see the miraculous. It is a waste of time to talk to them because dialogue will just lead to futile debate. When people are stuck in their human limitations, it's time to move forward with God's plans and let them witness God's deliverance.

So, we see Jesus going into action as He instructs the disciples to invite the people to sit down. Jesus didn't get mad at the disciples. He didn't punish them for their immaturity. He didn't say, "Because you lack faith, you won't get to be part of this miracle." Instead, Jesus took it upon Himself to keep going in God's plans and allowed His disciples to learn by seeing God work.

In feeding the people, the Apostle John tells us in John 6:11 that **Jesus then took the loaves, gave thanks, and distributed to those who were seated as much as they wanted. He did the same with the fish.**

Jesus was the one who handed out the bread with His own hands. Have you ever needed a direct touch from God?

Imagine someone sending you flowers through a courier. Now imagine they came in person and put the flowers in your hands. Imagine your hand touching theirs as they deliver the gift. Can you see the difference in the gift? Feel Jesus' hands touching your hands as He provides. When God sent Jesus, that's as personal as personal can get. God didn't send an angel. He didn't send a letter. He sent Himself through His one and only Son.

Do you need a direct touch from God today? Then let the story of Jesus personally handing out bread to the people encourage you in a special way.

John 6:11 tells us that Jesus was not afraid to give the people **"as much as they wanted."** He was the bread of life and He was sure of Himself and His ability to feed the people. He did not give with hesitance. He was not afraid to run out of bread. God is perfectly able to fulfill His role as Messiah!

Even though Jesus was the bread of life, He could have chosen to invite the disciples to distribute the bread with Him. Yet, He chose to do it Himself. Was it to send the message that only the Messiah is the bread of life? Or could it also be because God will not delegate the task of distributing resources to those who lack faith? People who have a scarcity mentality will always withhold blessings from others or they give in a way where they nickel and dime everything. The ones who understand God's plans and knows that God will provide is the one who will meet the need in the way God meets the need. God can't trust faithless people to be generous in the distribution of His provision!

If you have someone in the family or on your team who lacks faith, be careful not to assign them to any project that involves the distribution or sharing of resources. Those with little faith aren't the right choice to implement a God-sized mission. Only when we have the faith that God will provide will we then respond to the need of others with God's heart of generosity.

John 6:12–13 reads: **When they had all had enough to eat, he said to his disciples, "Gather the pieces that are left over. Let nothing be wasted." So they gathered them and filled twelve baskets with the pieces of the five barley loaves left over by those who had eaten.**

The disciples who didn't trust in Jesus as Messiah were not given the opportunity to distribute the resources.

Instead, John 6:12 tells us that after all the people **"had enough to eat"** the disciples were instructed to **"Gather the pieces that are left over."** God gave them the chance to feel and to touch the extra resources. As they filled up twelve baskets with the pieces of the five barley loaves God was showing them Jesus was the bread of life. As such, He has the capacity to feed all who come to Him. Those who lacked the faith to believe in the provision were given the chance to experience the overflow in the provision by picking up the leftovers!

MY APPLICATION

Jesus walked among the people as the bread of life and was completely able to feed those who came to Him. Today, Jesus still wants us to know that He is the bread of life. When God provides miraculously and trusts me with the distribution of His resources, I need to remember I am not giving out of my resources; I am giving out of His. I know I am influenced by my own lack of faith. If I have faith in God's sufficiency to provide for those in need, I find myself allocating funds generously. When I get fearful, I find myself rationing the resources. When I am in a period of faithlessness, I tell the staff never to ask me to approve any expense because the answer will be "No." It helps me to remember that my ability to provide comes from God's decision to give. My confidence in giving comes from knowing God desires to give to "these people" who are seeking Jesus. In John 6:2, God showed me that these people were among "a great crowd of people" who followed Jesus. This wasn't just any crowd; these were people who were specifically following Jesus.

Every year, Inspire Women awards scholarships and ministry grants. In spite of the economy, my assurance that God will provide the funds comes from knowing that the students are counted among "these people" who are seeking Jesus. Among all the different needs in our community, I can trust God to place priority on the needs of those who want more of Him.

YOUR APPLICATION

Describe a situation where you were faced with scarce resources. Share how you distributed resources according to God's priorities or if you distributed resources according to your personal priorities.

DAY 2

Devotion

WHEN GOD PROVIDES FOR OUR

PHYSICAL NEEDS, HIS ULTIMATE

GOAL IS TO FEED OUR SPIRITUAL

NEED—ARE YOU IN TUNE WITH

YOUR REAL NEED?

JOHN 6:14–15 READS: **After the people saw the miraculous sign that Jesus did, they began to say, "Surely this is the Prophet who is to come into the world." Jesus, knowing that they intended to come and make him king by force, withdrew again to a mountain by himself.** The people's statement shows us that God's purpose was accomplished. Moses was the prophet who fed the people in the desert with manna from heaven. The people recognized Jesus as being the greater prophet who fed them with miraculous bread. In John 6:14, it was **"After the people saw** the miraculous sign" that they recognized Jesus as "the Prophet who is to come into the world."

However, the breakdown happened right after the people acknowledged Jesus as the Messiah. They expected the Messiah to come as a king to overthrow the Roman Empire. So, the next thing they wanted to do was to crown Jesus as king. They never expected God to send Jesus as a servant. The people's expectations reveal their ignorance as to their real need. They saw themselves as righteous and deserving of a king who ruled the world. They regarded themselves as deserving of being citizens of a greater kingdom than Rome. They didn't see themselves as depraved and needing a Savior to pay the penalty of their sins.

What do you think is your real need? Have you set your heart on a big paycheck or a mansion? Have you dreamed of that perfect car? How do you view yourself and what you think you deserve? In what you expect God to give you, do you reveal your pride? Or does it reveal your humility and willingness to serve in whatever capacity God chooses for you?

My application

The people expected Jesus to be king because they felt they were worthy of a king. They didn't see that they needed a Messiah more than they needed a king. Their minds were filled with royalty and grandeur. They never imagined God would come as a servant.

I remember a time when I thought I was doing God a favor by laying down my career in corporate America. I was filled with arrogance and expected God to do great things through my life. I was surprised that God was silent. In that season of silence, I learned that God didn't need me. I learned that it was a privilege if I got to be involved in anything He was doing. As fast as God established me or any of my work, He could take away my health or my ability to think. I learned that any success I ever experienced was because of what God first poured into me. When God finally trusted me with His calling, I entered His service as a vessel fully aware that God didn't need me but, in His grace, allowed me to be part of His story.

YOUR APPLICATION

Describe a time you were confident of your talents and what you could offer God. Share how God humbled you and showed you it was your privilege to serve Him.

Day 3
Devotion

God reserves the right to

choose the way He solves

the problem—How have you

limited God by insisting on

your solution?

———

John 6:16–20 reads: **When evening came, his disciples went down to the lake, where they got into a boat and set off across the lake for Capernaum. By now it was dark, and Jesus had not yet joined them. A strong wind was blowing and the waters grew rough. When they had rowed three or three and a half miles, they saw Jesus approaching the boat, walking on the water; and they were terrified. But he said to them, "It is I; don't be afraid."**

Jesus allowed the disciples to row a good distance before He showed up. He also allowed the disciples to row in the dark. The exact distance wasn't the point. Rather, the point was simply that they were rowing for a while and in the dark. It probably felt like a lifetime. Then, all of a sudden, John 6:19b tells us the disciples saw Jesus approaching the boat, "walking on water."

Have you ever been in a place where you felt, "God could never get to me?" Perhaps you've felt lost in the dark. Perhaps you've felt forgotten. Perhaps you cannot imagine any plan that could possibly rescue you. Perhaps you cannot imagine your trial ever coming to an end. It was in this state of mind that the disciples witnessed God showing up with a solution that transcended human imagination.

If you were struggling in the middle of an ocean in modern times, you might be thinking along the lines of a helicopter showing up or a ship passing by. I doubt you would even think of God showing up and defying gravity by walking on water.

What does this teach us about God? He continues to demonstrate that He made the world and reserves the right to change the rules of gravity or whatever rules He established. God defied logic by feeding the five thousand with a few loaves and fish. He defied gravity to respond to the need of the disciples by walking to them on water. Have you limited God by your logic and lack of expectation?

It's normal to be terrified when we finally realize the person in our midst is God Himself. He's the all-powerful God who can use His power to save us. He's also the all-powerful God who can use His power to send us to eternal condemnation.

When Jesus showed up, announced that He was not coming in judgment, but as a friend. So, He said in John 6:20, "It is I; don't be afraid."

Have you been avoiding God because you've been fearful of what He would do to you for the choices you've made? Did you know God didn't send Jesus into the world to condemn the world, but to save it? God showing up is good news! Have you been avoiding good news? Is it time to welcome Jesus into your situation?

John 6:21 reads: **Then they were willing to take him into the boat, and immediately the boat reached the shore where they were heading.**

Are you willing to take Jesus into your boat? John 6:21 begins with the word "Then" to mark the exact time the disciples were willing to take Jesus into the boat. The "Then" was after Jesus told the disciples not to be afraid. Jesus first assured the disciples He was a safe friend. It was only then that they were willing to take Jesus into the boat. Did you need to be reminded today that Jesus is a safe friend?

As soon as Jesus entered the boat, John 6:21 tells us that **"immediately the boat reached the shore where they were heading."** Recall that the disciples had been rowing in the dark for a few miles. Recall that they were rowing against strong winds. Then they invited Jesus into their boat. They had to be willing to invite Jesus into the boat first before things could change. As soon as Jesus stepped into the boat, we are told that "immediately" the disciples "reached the shore." How did this happen?

There are times when God gives us the strength to keep rowing. Then there are times when God steps in and says, "Enough. You've arrived." God is the one who decides how long the journey will take. He can stop the sun to give you more time to fight the battle. **Joshua 10:12–13** tells us: **On the day the LORD gave the Amorites over to Israel, Joshua said to the LORD in the presence of Israel: "O sun, stand still over Gibeon, O moon, over the Valley of Aijalon." So the sun stood still, and the moon stopped, till the nation avenged itself on its enemies...**God can shorten the distance and give you supernatural speed and results. The key is to be willing to ask Jesus into your boat and then trust that, whatever happens, God is in control.

My application

God reserves the right to defy universal laws to respond to our needs. I remember a time God provided for the ministry in a way that surprised me. God brought someone into my life to play tennis with my dad. When I met with my dad's tennis partner for lunch, I didn't realize he was the answer to a need in the ministry. In a casual getting-to-know-you conversation, he told me he owned apartment buildings. At the time, I was looking for a way to support the staff payroll. Immediately, I sensed God prompting me to ask for an apartment. This friend said enthusiastically, "Just call my assistant." I asked what kind of apartment I could have. He said, "Whatever you want. You pick." I never imagined God would meet the need for payroll by taking care of housing for the staff.

When we invite God into our situation, He can then move freely to help our situation. When I was struggling with writing this book, I kept rewriting. My mind was so occupied with my grief that I could not keep my thoughts straight. The harder I worked, the less progress I made. Then I stopped and decided to ask God for help. In the past, I had never known my son to stop what he was doing to help me. He had just completed his internship with a law company and I knew he was tired. When I made my need known to him, he packed his backpack to leave for his apartment so he could focus on my manuscript. He left the house at three in the morning because he wanted to get started as soon as he could. He immersed himself in my manuscript. I knew without a doubt that God had intervened because this behavior was so unlike my son. God showed me that when He solves a problem, He can defy the odds and use personalities we never imagined to be part of the solution.

YOUR APPLICATION

Describe a need you struggled with. Share how you may have limited God by specifying the way the need could be met instead of letting God solve the problem His way. Or share a time you didn't invite God into your situation because of fear. What were you afraid of?

DAY 4

Devotion

WHEN GOD HAS LEFT A

LOCATION, HIS ABSENCE WILL

BE EVIDENT—HAVE YOU

STAYED BEHIND WHEN GOD HAS

ALREADY LEFT?

———◆———

John 6:22–24 reads: **The next day the crowd that had stayed on the opposite shore of the lake realized that only one boat had been there, and that Jesus had not entered it with his disciples, but that they had gone away alone. Then some boats from Tiberias landed near the place where the people had eaten the bread after the Lord had given thanks. Once the crowd realized that neither Jesus nor his disciples were there, they got into the boats and went to Capernaum in search of Jesus.**

John 6:22b tells us that the people observed that **"only one boat had been there and that Jesus had not entered it."** If the disciples left in the only boat that was there, and if Jesus had not entered it, then the question was, "Where was Jesus?" All the crowd knew was that He didn't enter the boat. They finally went looking for Him.

Have you ever been in a place where you no longer sensed God's presence? How much do you want to follow God? There are times you may never understand what happened to His presence; you just know it's not present anymore. The question is, will you stay where you are without God's presence or will you search for Him? Will you leave wherever you are in order to find more of God?

When you finally catch up with God, what do you think you'll find? Many times our focus is material, whereas God is more interested in our eternal salvation and rewards.

John 6:25–27 reads: **When they found him on the other side of the lake, they asked him, "Rabbi, when did you get here?" Jesus answered, "I tell you the truth, you are looking for me, not because you saw miraculous signs but because you ate the loaves and had your fill. Do not work for food that spoils, but for food that endures to eternal life, which the Son of Man will give you. On him God the Father has placed his seal of approval."**

When the crowd found Jesus, they said in John 6:25b, **"Rabbi, when did you get here?"** Jesus never answered the question. God doesn't owe us an explanation as to where He is working or when He will leave one place to go to another. What Jesus wanted was for the people to recognize the need within them that caused them to look for Him. He wanted them to see that they were not chasing the sensational. They were not just looking for a miracle. Instead, something filled their lives in a way that no earthly provision could. Jesus wanted them to graduate to the next level of faith. No longer should they be chasing temporary material provision but God's eternal provision.

Our human tendency is to focus on the temporary earthly provision. It's to live for the next miracle like a child demanding God to entertain us. When we have personally experienced God filling our soul with His truth, He expects us to want what is eternal. Jesus tells the people in John 6:27a, **"Do not work for food that spoils, but for food that endures to eternal life, which the Son of Man will give you."**

When God provides materially, it's never an end in itself. Perhaps you have gotten a job, perhaps God has blessed your business, perhaps someone miraculously gave you the funds you needed. Your physical provision is never God's end objective. His provision is always to get our attention so He can lead us to spiritual food. God lives on an eternal timeline. He wants to give us more than temporary success on earth. He wants our eternal salvation.

If you are consumed with physical needs to the point that you've thrown God's mission out of your life, then you've returned to working for **"food that spoils"** when what God wants to give you is **"food that endures to eternal life."**

John 6:30 reads: **So they asked him, "What miraculous sign then will you give that we may see it and believe you? What will you do?"**

No matter what Jesus did, it seemed like the crowd was always asking for one more sign. How many of us create delay in our lives because we want God to show us one more thing? Jesus wanted them to know that *He* was the sign. He was the bread of life that God was giving to feed the people.

The truth of God being the provision is something the human mind struggles with. We tend to want the physical blessings God can give instead of appreciating His person. But God and His blessings are one. God and His mission are one. Have you been guilty of loving the blessings without loving God?

MY APPLICATION

When the people followed God, He led them to spiritual blessings. I remember a season in my life when God gave me a physical provision. I immediately wanted God to show me how He would provide for the next need. God had to teach me to savor the moment and cherish the true miracle. The miracle wasn't in the physical need being met. The true miracle was in the fact that the God of the universe looked my way and used me to take care of a need in the community. I learned that when we park on the wrong provision, we go from sensation to sensation. But when we recognize that God wants a relationship with us and is building His kingdom on earth through us, we bask in a relationship that surpasses any human relation. He fills our heart to overflow.

At Inspire Women, those in the leadership development program are required to trust God for part of their support. There are months when their basic stipend can hardly cover their expenses. Then, one day, a donor granted the ministry's request to provide permanent housing for the staff. This way, they could always be assured of a roof over their heads.

On July 12, 2011 Inspire Women's La Misericordia House of Mercy was established in memory of Eleanor "Puddie" Pitcock. The gift came as a surprise for my birthday. This residence was provided by the generosity of Mr. Doug Pitcock, the CEO of Williams Brothers, to house servants who share God's mercy with the world. When God provided this housing, one of the interns broke into worship. The praises from her mouth embraced these words, "Oh, God, I wish I could sacrifice more for you! I am in awe of your goodness. Thank you for taking care of the needs of those who serve you." She was grateful for the roof over her head. She couldn't thank Mr. Pitcock enough for his gift. Best of all, she was in awe of God's person and goodness to protect those who served Him.

YOUR APPLICATION

Describe a time you became consumed with material possessions and physical provision. Test your heart by listing your greatest treasure. Now say whether you would be willing to give it away if God asked you for it. Share how you can focus on your relationship with God in order to redirect your focus to the real blessing.

Day 5

Devotion

Even well intentioned

individuals struggled

with following God—

We need God's help to

continue with Him.

John 6:28–29 reads: **Then they asked him, "What must we do to do the works God requires?" Jesus answered, "The work of God is this: to believe in the one he has sent."**

The people said in John 6:28, **"What must we do to do the works God requires?"** Their mindset was in doing. They were filled with confidence in their own strength. What God was asking for wasn't works from the flesh of fallen humanity. God's plan required the people to trust in His provision.

John 6:34–35 reads: **"Sir," they said, "from now on give us this bread." Then Jesus declared, "I am the bread of life. He who comes to me will never go hungry, and he who believes in me will never be thirsty."**

The people said in John 6:34b to, **"give us this bread,"** referring to a physical provision of bread. They were still looking for a provision that was outside of the person of Jesus.

John 6:36 reads: **"But as I told you, you have seen me and still you do not believe."**

Jesus was saying that the person of God was standing right in front of them, and they still did not believe. God wasn't asking them to believe someone who was distant or remote. He came down from heaven to be right in their midst.

John 6:60–62 reads: **On hearing it, many of his disciples said, "This is a hard teaching. Who can accept it?" Aware that his disciples were grumbling about this, Jesus said to them, "Does this offend you? What if you see the Son of Man ascend to where he was before?"**

Even those close to Jesus struggled with what He was saying. We see Jesus being sensitive to those closest to him and offered them evidence that His message was true. Jesus planted the seed for what He knew His disciples would witness in the future. He said in John 6:62, **"What if you see the Son of Man ascend to where he was before?"** Oh, the grace of God to keep giving us evidence so we can believe!

In your life, has someone spoken a word of truth in your life years ago that is now coming to pass? Don't miss the evidence and confirmation of being in the middle of a prophecy coming true in your life.

John 6:64b-66 reads: **For Jesus had known from the beginning which of them did not believe and who would betray him. From this time many of his disciples turned back and no longer followed him.**

In John 6:64, Jesus knew that, in addition to Judas' betrayal, there would be others who **"did not believe."** Have you ever tried to explain God's plan to those around you? Instead of focusing on a "Judas" in your midst, learn from Jesus in John 6:66b that there were others who **"no longer followed him."**

These others who no longer followed Jesus weren't betrayers. They could've been well-intentioned individuals. They were simply followers who couldn't make it with God to the next level. If you have experienced followers or friends who couldn't journey with you into the next level of your journey with God, nothing unusual has happened. Instead of feeling betrayed, understand the dynamics of a journey with God. Not everyone will be able to hang in there with you or continue with you when the teaching gets difficult and defies human logic. That's why Jesus went on to say in John 6:65, **"This is why I told you that no one can come to me unless the Father has enabled him."**

Jesus was telling His followers that their ability to get to the next level of faith can only be with the Father's help. The problem was the people did not think they needed help. In their self-righteousness, they depended on themselves. As a result, they missed out on continuing with God in their journey.

Those who no longer followed Him were not Jesus' inner circle. When a leader sees the attrition from the crowd, the focus turns inward. So, Jesus said to His disciples in John 6:67, **"You do not want to leave too, do you?"**

Every leader should take a pulse on the heartbeat of those closest to them. Are they still on board or do they have one foot out the door? Simon Peter rose to the occasion and committed to stay with Jesus. He said in John 6:68–69, **"Lord, to whom shall we go? You have the words of eternal life. We believe and know that you are the Holy One of God."**

The question of "Who's with me?" isn't for the leader but for the followers to assess their convictions. Jesus wasn't asking because He needed the support. Jesus kept going in God's mission no matter what the opinions were around Him. What God wants to know is, "Are you following?" Whether or not people follow does not change the fact. Jesus is the Messiah and the bread of life God sent to save the world.

MY APPLICATION

Jesus wants us to trust Him as our bread of life. I find I cannot trust by trying to trust in my own power. Even in trusting, I need God to help me to trust. The tension between God and me is the battle for control. I want to control my provision. God wants me to trust Him for it. To depend on God for my life puts me in a dependent position. It requires me to get close to Him. There are times I find myself avoiding God because getting too close makes me nervous. In the ministry I oversee, there are times I invite staff members into my confidence.

What I have discovered is that some people like the distance. They don't want to be too close to the leader because they want to manage their own time. They don't want to know more about the inner workings of the ministry for fear it will require more from them. They want a balanced life where they can have their own lives and fit the ministry around their personal schedules. In watching them, I see myself in how I relate to God. There are times I avoid the idea of Jesus being the bread of life. The idea of God being my sustenance feels too intimate for comfort. For God to be my only sustenance is like having my heart beat as one with my Creator. The only way I can get comfortable with this closeness is when I determine that I have no life except for through God's Son. Do I really believe that any life outside of God's will is a waste of time and will count for nothing in eternity?

Your application

Describe a time you had to trust God for your provision. Share your emotions during this time. How did depending on God make you less confident? Do you trust yourself more than God?

WEEKEND
Reflection

MY APPLICATION

As I lead the ministry of Inspire Women forward, my heart feels settled over reconciling my losses and trusting God with the future. My new concern is the looming reports of the economy and how the financial state of our country will impact God's ministries.

Like Philip, who told Jesus there was no human way he could meet the need of the crowds, I find myself helpless against factors outside of my control. In the midst of economic uncertainty, God showed me the only question I need to answer is whether I am doing His will. If I'm in His will, then my security is in knowing that He will provide.

There's freedom in throwing off the platter all that is not God's will. It's definitely a way to de-clutter. It is also a sure way to identify what really matters. There are so many things in our lives that don't matter for eternity. Sometimes I wonder if God allowed the economic challenge so we can get clarity as to what are the essentials and what are the "nice to haves." Jesus is the bread of life. He has the capacity to provide for all who come to Him for eternal life. He also has the capacity to meet the need of all plans according to God's will and timing.

YOUR APPLICATION

Describe a time you had enough resources to take care of a need. Then take a quick inventory of your assets as of today and how a health or economic crisis could deplete your resources. State how you would have responded in the past to a challenge to your resources and how you would respond today based on what you learned from this chapter.

Epilogue

When life gives you a hundred reasons to cry, show
life that you have a thousand reasons to smile.

—*Anonymous*

W HAT EMOTIONAL STATE WERE you in when you picked up this book?

Let me share mine with you. I praise God for comforting me while I was writing. By the time I typed the last word, I felt a sense of completion. I had discovered renewed passion to finish the dream.

I pray the insights God gave me through the Book of John and other Scriptures can help anyone to make more sense of life, no matter what he or she is dealing with. For me, I was struggling with what it meant to continue a challenging mission without my spiritual father and mother. God brought my spiritual father home to him after struggling with Alzheimer's disease for five years. The year I lost my spiritual father, my spiritual mother was diagnosed with the same disease.

When I reflect over the years of my life, I recall my first loss was a puppy. A friend counseled me to immediately get another one. I was surprised at how the new puppy helped tremendously in taking away that feeling of missing my first puppy. However, when I lost my first best friend, life didn't move on as quickly. There are some people who just aren't replaceable. God never meant them to be. They were a gift for a season, and their devotion to us will forever remain a lasting source of strength.

The last time I called my spiritual mother, I braced myself for a short conversation. I had prepared myself to hear, "I'm in pain," followed by a quick goodbye and the click of the phone. In the twelve years of our friendship, she used to keep me on the phone. When I had to go, she would say, "Call me back." These days she hangs up quickly. So, I was surprised when she said, "How are you, dear? Would you like to come over?" I picked up my bag and rushed out the door. I prayed that things would not have changed by the time I got to her house. Please, God, let her stay aware of her surroundings for at least a few minutes after I get there.

God answered my prayers. She was her normal self for at least ten minutes after I arrived. Her melodious voice was light and cheerful. She stroked my face lightly and said, "My sweet Anita, I love you so much." I told her, "I love you too." She answered, "I love you more." Then she said, "I have to go lay down now. Is that all right?" I said, "Sure," and watched her walk away with her caretaker. As I drove home, I told myself, "This was a good day. Not because she spoke to me or because she remembered me or because she smiled at me. This was a good day because Christ is my comfort." His is the voice I will listen for. My ears are tuned to a constant source of comfort and guidance for my future.

I will discern the right voice to follow.

The Devil is God's enemy and desires to get back at God by destroying His children. If the Devil was designing a torpedo to strike at my heart, he definitely did his research and custom-tailored the perfect weapon. He knew about the emotional wounds from my childhood. He was perfectly aware of my issues with abandonment. How clever of him to design an illness that would prolong the process of abandonment by repeating the hellos and goodbyes. God reminded me that He wasn't oblivious to my past. He knew about my vulnerabilities as well. God could have prevented the Devil from opening up my childhood wounds. Yet, God wasn't afraid of the attack. Instead, God wanted me to overcome with His truth. The fact is, no matter what my background, I no longer live in the past. I now belong in God's family tree.

I will resolve a father or mother wound.

Life is filled with hellos and goodbyes. I prefer hellos because they are filled with hope and new expectation. The goodbyes I prefer to fast forward. There are times I find myself afraid to get too close to people because it takes courage to love. It takes courage to feel. Granted, life would be flat without love. On the other hand, it would also be so much less painful. On looking back on my life, I don't know if it was easier to say goodbye to my biological mother when she exited abruptly from my life as compared to the long goodbye to my spiritual mother because of her illness. A friend of mine said her mother's Alzheimer's disease lasted for twenty-five years. I don't know how long my spiritual mother will endure. I don't even try to project the number of days she has left. I just know that, even in the delay, God is working out His purpose. There are times a long goodbye is necessary to reveal the hearts of loved ones. I know that on the other side of eternity, my spiritual mother will see how many people loved her, even when she couldn't love them back. When I'm rushing God to make everything right immediately, whose agenda am I serving? God cannot be pushed. He serves His own purpose. He is never in a hurry because all things will be perfected in His time.

I will trust God's timing has a reason.

For the past twelve years, God chose to develop me as a leader by assigning me a spiritual father and a spiritual mother as two personal coaches who were devoted to me. However, seasons change, and God reserves the right to change the way He works. Although it may seem like He is removing some pillars in my life, He is actually teaching me to soar higher with the empowerment of His Spirit. He is showing me that He was the one who has been with me from the beginning, and He will continue with me to eternity. God has a master plan for the world and for my life. For where God wants to take me, my spiritual father and mother didn't have the strength or capability to continue with me. God will protect His own mission by assigning the appropriate personnel to complete the team. For the next part of the journey, God will draw others closer to me to complement my weaknesses. He did so with my Board members and with my staff. I don't believe it was coincidental that my husband retired earlier than he had expected and began volunteering full time in the ministry. God is the perfect navigation system. He can change the plan to get to the goal. He definitely changed the personnel plan! No matter how many detours, He can re-plot the map. His ultimate goal is to announce, "You have arrived at your destination."

I will release plans that no longer work.

There are days I will miss those who walked so closely with me. For example, my spiritual father always encouraged me to keep going and to keep growing the ministry. Not only did he believe God had called me, but he helped me to believe in God's divine appointment for my life.

My spiritual mother was my confidante. I could trust her with all my emotional drama and the private details of my life. She would never share any of my information with a living soul. She would even warn me of who I shouldn't trust. In all the twelve years she walked with me, she never once raised her voice. The most upset I saw her was when she was

aggravated with me for wanting to build bridges with someone who was jealous of me. She insisted I had no chance of
succeeding, I insisted I should try. To show her disapproval,
she said, "If you do this, I will stop praying for you!" Then
she immediately recanted and said, "Okay, I will keep praying." And I would say, "If I get hurt, I need you to help me
through it!" And she would say, "Of course, I will."

If I tried to find someone to be to me what my spiritual father and mother were, I would be setting myself up for
disappointment. No one can ever take the place of someone so unique and God-appointed. What I need to do is
to count the good years and thank God for them. Not everyone is privileged to have had spiritual parents who loved
them so completely and wanted them to succeed. Even if I
never experience this kind of devotion again, what God has
given me is the extreme love I have received from His one
and only Son. The world was offered a Savior, but not everyone chose to receive Him as God's greatest gift. Thank
God I chose Jesus! So I will redirect my focus to Him. He
came to earth to secure my way to heaven. He refused to
leave before He had paid in full the penalty for my sins. He
is the one who will continue with me for the rest of my life
till eternity. From the overflow in my heart, I will continue
to share God's hope with the world. In Jesus,

I will discover emotional fulfillment.

Some people pound on the gates of heaven and never hear
an answer. They give up on God and try to find their answers elsewhere. Then there are those who have lived with

their pain for so long they don't even expect an answer. When God shows up, it's like having Christmas in the middle of July. I know God didn't answer me because I deserved an answer. I can only surmise that it must have fit His purpose to offer me an answer. I don't need to know why. I just know I'm grateful for how God showed me that, while my spiritual mother's body is getting weaker, her spirit is getter stronger. So, in a way, she is getting better every day until she reaches perfection in mind, spirit, and body.

I will settle those lingering questions. (Thank God I didn't have to wait for years!)

With illnesses often come additional expenses. Illnesses have a way of depleting us financially, physically, and emotionally. There were days I was running on fumes. There were other days I was running on empty. Yet, miraculously, God has a way of stretching the resources. He has a way of bringing provision through unexpected sources. Through an email, a letter, a phone call with great news, God astounds me with His creativity. When I most needed divine intervention, God led a friend of the ministry to surprise me with a birthday gift. Though the gift was monetary, it meant more to me than that. I needed something radical to happen to assure me that God was continuing with me with the same divine favor as I experienced while journeying with my spiritual father and mother. I needed to be assured that His hand was still on my life. The gift of establishing Inspire Women's residence for the staff was God's assurance to me that He is still working even when He was allowing some pillars in my life to be removed. He was reminding me that He still lives even if He allows others to be brought home to Him. Best of all, He lives within my heart. In God, I have found my sufficiency and supply.

I will trust God to provide for His dreams.

So, where am I after typing the last word of *Making Sense of Your Life?* I am not staring at a five year business plan or putting my hopes in any one individual. My security is in Jesus. I will listen to His voice. I will find my security in Him as my ultimate parent and find my roots in being in His faith family. I will trust His timing to perfect me and those around me. I will stop grieving what used to be and release what will no longer get me to my destination. I will trust God as the only one who can take me to the next level. I will look to Jesus to complete my emotional needs. I find myself settled in the questions that I wrestled with over Alzheimer's disease. Finally, I am confident that when I am in God's will, He has the capacity to provide for all His plans. In all the above, I believe I am in a place where I have made more sense of my life. What about you?

ABOUT ANITA CARMAN

ANITA CARMAN was born in Hong Kong when it was under British rule. She came to America at the age of seventeen, after her mother's tragic suicide. Uprooted from her family and country, she desperately searched for purpose. She never imagined God would establish her as the founder of a ministry to help thousands live out His purpose.

Anita's childhood memories of seeing women degraded fueled a passion to educate women to reach their potential. Her mother's loss made her more determined to help women finish God's dreams and not allow setbacks to discourage them. A local pastor once told Anita, "God called you to be a burden carrier." Anita embraces the dreams of other women to serve God in missions and ministry and works tirelessly to empower them to fulfill that passion.

Anita served as a leader in Bible teacher and bestselling author Beth Moore's Sunday school class for seven years, and Beth called on Anita to teach in her absence. One day, Beth challenged her to leave the protection of her class and soar with God, saying,

"Anita, you have the cloak. Just dip it in the water." Anita left Beth's class to serve for five years at one of the largest multi-ethnic Bible colleges in the country. She began as Director of Women's Ministry and became the Vice President of Special Programs and Special Assistant to the President. Although she longed to serve in an established organization, God invited Anita to go into uncharted territory. She left the college in 2003 to implement God's vision to empower His daughters.

Today, Anita is the founder and president of Inspire Women, a 501(c) 3 non-profit organization that inspires thousands of God's daughters to serve at their potential. Its year-round program identifies and develops leaders for missions and ministry. Through Anita's leadership, Inspire Women reaches over 100,000 annually through radio programs, publications, and Houston-based outreaches. The ministry mentors over 600 ministry leaders a year and funds 50-70 scholarships and ministry grants. Since its formation a decade ago, Inspire Women has invested over $1,000,000 to train leaders to shape and to work in a multitude of ministries. Women reach the abused, the homeless, suicidal teens, at-risk youth, trafficked children, recovering addicts, divorcees, widows, and all others who need God's hope and message.

Anita has been recognized often in her adopted hometown. The NBC news affiliate featured Anita as "Houston's most inspiring woman," while FOX 26 highlighted how Anita was changing the city andWB-39 featured Anita in their "unsung heroes" segment. The Daughters of the American Revolution have also honored Anita as an immigrant who changed America.

Anita is a sought-after speaker in conferences and churches. To invite Anita Carman to speak at your next event go to www. inspirewomen.org or call 713-521-3424

About Robbie Carman

ROBERT CARMAN (Robbie) is Anita Carman's oldest son. After graduating from Cornell University with a degree in engineering, he came back to Texas to pursue a law degree at the University of Texas.

A long-time encourager and motivator of his mom, he often quoted Scripture to her at times when she needed the peace and clarity that God's word offers. One of his favorites was Ecclesiastes 9:11, which states that in this world, "the race is not to the swift, nor the battle to the strong…but time and chance happen to them all." God's wisdom taught Robbie that life is about running the race till you cross the finish line. His contribution to this book was a gift from a son to his mother.

He plans to move back to Houston to practice corporate law. In his spare time, he enjoys basketball, practicing taekwondo, playing the guitar, and debating theological questions.

Inspire! ™
WOMEN

Investing in Women who
Change the World

Our Mission:
    To inspire women of all ethnicities to serve at their potential with year-round programs to develop leaders for missions and ministry and to fund scholarships and ministry grants.

TRAINING FOR EVERY SEASON OF LIFE

Our Programs:
    Anita Carman's publications and radio programs reach thousands globally. Her weekly e-devotion stirs women to flourish in God's power and love. Life-changing stories and challenges fill her books: *When Dreams Won't Die, Transforming for a Purpose,* and *Making Sense of Your Life.* Anita can be heard daily on FM105.7 KHCB radio and other stations across the nation.

    Our scholarships fund training in accredited seminaries and specialized programs, and our grants provide resources to mobilize ministry and extend impact.

Our citywide events in Houston rally thousands of women annually as we search for individuals who desire to serve in missions or ministry at their God-given potential.

Our Inner Circles are monthly gatherings at Inspire Women's spiritual oasis for those with leadership or shepherding responsibilities in need of spiritual replenishment. Over 600 leaders attend every year.

Our Leadership Institute develops leaders to have the spiritual fortitude to define, pursue, and finish God's mission. This accredited program includes instruction, mentoring, individually designed projects, and ministry grants to put faith into action.

For more information on Inspire Women's programs or to make a donation to help train women for ministry visit us at www.inspirewomen.org or call 713-521-1400.

Donations can be mailed to Inspire Women 1415 S.Voss Rd. #110-516 Houston, TX 77057.

ALSO BY ANITA CARMAN

TRANSFORMING FOR A PURPOSE:

Fulfilling God's Mission as Daughters of the King

As daughters of the King of Kings, our emotions should reflect our confidence in Him, right?

That's easier said than done. Anita Carman knows how debilitating three particular emotions—loneliness, rejection, and fear—can be. But she also knows the power of Jesus Christ.

As Anita writes, "Throughout this book, you will be led to look into God's Word to discover how to transform your emotions for God's purpose, using His counsel and the experiences of His people." In down-to-earth fashion, she walks us through the emotions that taint our thinking and keep us from experiencing God's desires for us. She adds: "Our ability (or inability) to flow with the changes in our lives comes from our belief (or unbelief) in the goodness of the Change Agent Himself."

Transforming for a Purpose will challenge the way you live—and who you really believe in. "A person who lives by faith is one who intentionally models her behavior after the faith heroes in the Bible and trusts that making such a choice is the best choice, no matter what the outcome." Radical? Maybe. Biblical? Definitely.

Don't let loneliness, rejection, or fear sabotage your dreams any longer. Be transformed today.

Copyright 2009
Published by Moody Publishers
Available from your favorite bookstore or online at
www.inspirewomen.org